Evil Hour in Colombia

FORREST HYLTON

VERSO
London • New York

In memory of Michael F. Jiménez (1948–2001)

First published by Verso 2006
© Forrest Hylton 2006
All rights reserved

The moral rights of the author have been asserted

1 3 5 7 9 10 8 6 4 2

Verso
UK: 6 Meard Street, London W1F 0EG
USA: 180 Varick Street, New York, NY 10014–4606
www.versobooks.com

Verso is the imprint of New Left Books

ISBN-13: 978-1-84467-072-7 (hbk)
ISBN-10: 1-84467-072-4

ISBN-13: 978-1-84467-551-7 (pbk)
ISBN-10: 1-84467-551-3

British Library Cataloguing in Publication Data
A catalogue record for this book is available from the British Library

Library of Congress Cataloging-in-Publication Data
A catalog record for this book is available from the Library of Congress

Typeset in Garamond by Hewer Text UK Ltd, Edinburgh
Printed in the UK by Bath Press

Contents

Caribbean
Sea

Sierra Nevada
de Santa Marta

Santa Marta

Barranquilla

GUAJIRA

MAGDALENA

ATLÁNTICO

BOLÍVAR

CÉSAR

PANAMA

Urabá

SUCRE

CÓRDOBA

R. Cauca

NORTE DE
SANTANDER

VENEZUELA

Pacific
Ocean

ANTIOQUIA

Magdalena Medio

Barrancabermeja

Medellín

SANTANDER

Puerto Berrío

ARAUCA

CHOCÓ

CALDAS

BOYACÁ

CASANARE

RISARALDA

Líbano

CUNDINA-
MARCA

VICHADA

Pereira

QUINDÍO

TOLIMA

Bogotá

COLOMBIA

Buenaventura

Cali

R. Magdalena

Villavicencio

SANTAFÉ DE BOGOTÁ

VALLE

Marquetalia

META

GUAINÍA

CAUCA

HUILA

Uribe

San José
del Guaviare

NARIÑO

Florencia

GUAVIARE

R. Vaupés

PUTUMAYO

CAQUETÁ

VAUPÉS

R. Caquetá

ECUADOR

R. Putumayo

AMAZONAS

BRAZIL

PERU

R. Amazon

Main colonization zones
since 1940

Leticia

0 ━━━━━━ 200 Miles

Acknowledgments

Thanks to Perry Anderson, Anne Beech, Robin Blackburn, Leslie Gill, Greg Grandin, Nivedita Menon, Arzoo Orsanloo, Christian Parenti, Raúl Prada, Marcus Rediker, Emir Sader, Jamie Sanders, and Danny Widener, as well as Susan Watkins and Tony Wood at *New Left Review*, for suggestions, support, and/or criticisms at different stages of writing. Tariq Ali had the idea of turning the *New Left Review* essay into a book, and Tom Penn at Verso patiently helped me get it to press. Thanks to Alison Austen for her care and thoroughness in copy-editing. Peter Linebaugh gave good advice early on, as did Aijaz Ahmad towards the end. Mike Davis pushed the project from the beginning; without his encouragement, it would likely have remained unpublished. Steele, my son, wanted to help me finish, and gave me good reason to do so. Gonzalo Sánchez corrected mistakes, helped with bibliography, rescued me from (some) pitfalls of pamphleteering, and explained how the conditions in which Colombian intellectuals live shape their work. Errors of fact and interpretation, of course, are mine.

The book grew out of a talk in October 2002 on the theme of state terror, organized by graduate students in the American Studies Department at New York University. I am grateful to Peter Hudson for taking the initiative, and to my co-speaker Garry Leech for enlarging my understanding of frontier settlers in the coca economy. In April 2006, I was fortunate to discuss the introduction and several early chapters of the book with participants in the *Culture, Power, Boundaries* seminar at Columbia University; at the International Center for Advanced Studies seminar at New York University, I discussed the introduction and several later chapters. The History Department and ICAS at NYU made reading, writing, and travel materially possible, although it took far too much time away from dissertation research and writing. Thanks to Sinclair Thomson and Tim Mitchell for their patience.

I owe an unpayable debt to Colombian lawyers, journalists, human rights and trade union activists, feminist activists, neighborhood organizers, students, and professors. Their insights in formal interviews and informal conversations forced me to view things afresh each time I visited. Their irrepressible sense of humor, like their steadfast commitment to humane principles – frequently in the face of life-threatening danger – continues to be a source of inspiration.

List of Acronyms

AAA:	American Anti-communist Alliance
ACCU:	Peasant Self-Defense Forces of Córdoba and Urabá
ANAPO:	National Popular Alliance
ANDI:	National Industrialists' Association
ANUC:	National Association of Peasant Users
AUC:	United Self-Defense Forces
BCB:	Central Bolívar Bloc of AUC
BCN:	Cacique Nutibara Bloc of AUC
BN:	Northern Bloc of AUC
CGSB:	Simón Bolívar Guerrilla Coordination
CRIC:	Cauca Regional Indigenous Council
CTC:	Colombian Workers' Confederation
ELN:	National Liberation Army
EPL:	People's Liberation Army
FARC:	Colombian Revolutionary Armed Forces
FEDECAFE:	Coffee Growers' Federation
FEDEGAN:	Federation of Cattle Ranchers
FEDENAL:	National Federation of Transport Workers
FENALCO:	National Coffee Growers' Federation
M-19:	April 19 Movement
MAS:	Death to Kidnappers
MRL:	Revolutionary Liberal Movement
ONIC:	Colombian National Indigenous Organization
PCC:	Colombian Communist Party
PCC-ML:	Colombian Communist Party-Marxist-Leninist (Maoist)
PRT:	Revolutionary Workers' Party (Trotskyist)

PSD: Social Democratic Party: name of PCC from mid-
                1940s through early 1950s
PSR: Revolutionary Socialist Party
SAC: Colombian Agriculturalists' Association
UNIR: National Union of the Revolutionary Left
UP: Patriotic Union
USO: Oil Workers' Union
UTC: Catholic Workers' Union

Prologue

Gonzalo Sánchez, Professor Emeritus of History, Universidad Nacional de Colombia, Bogotá

This book is the product of enchantment – the enchantment with Colombia of this young North American scholar who divides his research between the Colombia of Álvaro Uribe and the Bolivia of Evo Morales.

The author's intellectual debt – expressed in the brief correspondence I have had with him – determines, to a large extent, his perspective. Formed by British social history (Eric Hobsbawm, E.P. Thompson, Christopher Hill), South Asian subaltern studies (Ranajit Guha, Partha Chatterjee), and the critical eye of Edward Said, Forrest Hylton's enchantment led him to search for the logic – or, if you like, the critique – of the reasons for Colombian conflict. Despite his militant spirit, the search left him with the sensation that Colombian history is dominated by an insuperable oscillation between the emergence of radical-popular demands and protest and the following wave of repression – the inevitable response to which was armed rebellion. Perhaps armed rebellion, via recurrence, translates into what the author calls the "military hypertrophy" of resistance. This is at least one of the knots that this weighty, militant book reveals.

It is, I repeat, a product of enchantment, but also disenchantment: the author's disenchantment with the vagueness of approaches to violence that have become generalized and according to which violence has nothing to do with the socioeconomic situation, the closure of the political system, or the poverty that comparative statistics daily reveal. Devoid of explanation, we have become mute in the face of a type of privileging of what we might call the immateriality of violence. This text is a refutation of, and a vigorous response to, this emptying of reason and sense, and represents a clear search for the substance of the Colombian conflict.

In the development of the text, there are three elements, or thematic blocks, that stand out over the long term (*longue durée*). The first is the specific form, during the nineteenth century, of the construction of a political order. In reality, elites have been as fragmented as the country's topography, but forces contesting them have not escaped this fragmentation either – whether trade unions, peasant organizations, guerrillas, or political fronts. In this context, the "oligarchic democracy" based on bipartisanism has been maintained with violence, but without the institutional leaps that led, in other countries, to populism, agrarian social revolutions, or military dictatorships. Further, radical-popular republicanism, which had a vigorous, promising burst between 1849 and 1854, and which, according to the author, put Colombia at the vanguard of liberal reformism and republican political mobilization in the Atlantic world, was disarticulated, first with the Regeneration, and again in the mid-twentieth century with *la Violencia*. Additionally, although the author does not disregard ideological affiliations, he goes against the grain of a tradition that has paid particular attention to them, since he is more interested in the practices, rituals, and everyday politics of *los de abajo* (those from below: indigenous, artisans, Afro-Colombians, frontier settlers, and peasant communities). This gives an especially dynamic stamp to the changing scenes this important text describes and analyzes.

The second thematic axis refers to the dynamics of the social order, which, beginning in the nineteenth century, have revolved around land struggles and the processes of migration and settlement in the countryside and from country to city, as well as fruitless attempts to break with bipartisan clientelism. After repeated ups and downs of reform and violence, on the cusp of the millennium the social architecture culminates with a crushing agrarian counter-reform – a modern re-feudalization of the countryside by paramilitaries and narcotraffickers – that not only represents the expropriation-concentration of property, but the reversion of democratic processes and gains of preceding decades. This involves the reconfiguration of hegemonies and exclusions in a large number of departments (the territorial divisions of Colombia).

The third nucleus of arguments asks about the structuring of power and violence, from the 1950s until now, in a situation of competition between the limited sovereignty of the state and the concurrent pretensions to sovereignty on the part of insurgents and counterinsurgents – a concurrence the weightiest result of which is the privatization of coercive power.

Of course, this privatization, which is enormously decentralized, brings other consequences along with it: the privatization of violence darkened the frontier between civilians and combatants in Colombia long before Michael Ignatieff's brilliant *The Warrior's Honor* signaled it as one of the characteristics of contemporary wars. Presidents like Laureano Gómez in the 1950s, and César Turbay Ayala with his "Security Statute" at the end of the 1970s, find their cold war accents echoed today under President Álvaro Uribe Vélez's "democratic security" policies. The moments are of course distinguishable, but there is something that all these regimes, including the present, share: an irrepressible repugnance for ideas like civil resistance, peace communities or territories, indigenous neutrality, and, in general, any type of separation from the armed forces. The population is seen either as the extension of the army or the insurgency.

Echoing Hobsbawm's findings – "I discovered a country in which the failure to make a social revolution had made violence the constant, universal, and omnipresent core of public life" – perhaps it can be said that for the author of *Evil Hour in Colombia*, the history of Colombia has involved the stubborn containment of a profound demand for social revolution; a social revolution that was defeated first by the Regeneration after the Age of Capital, at the end of the nineteenth century; aborted after the Second World War, especially during *la Violencia* of the 1950s; and, finally, truncated by the collapse of the Soviet Union, the crisis of really existing socialism, and the involution of revolutionary cycles in Central America. Between each historical cycle of revolution-counter-revolution, there have been brief reformist interludes.

Of course the consequences of this historical trajectory are long-lasting. The mentalities of a country that has had a revolution, even if it was later interrupted (as in the cases of Mexico and Nicaragua), are not the same as those in a country which has proven unable to make one. In the first case, the exercise of popular power, even in passing, left an enormous confidence in the transformative capacity of collective action, while a profound historical pessimism about the possibility of radical change has been accentuated in the second, the case of Colombia. This would also explain why, in Colombia, memory as trauma weighs so heavily on memory as heroic celebration.

Obviously this is not a question of evidence, pure and simple. Such singularity turns out to be comprehensible only within the framework of careful historical reflection. The question "Where are we?" is only clarified for us to the extent that we can establish structural determinants, meaning an answer to the question, "Where do we come from?" It is true that during the nineteenth century, Colombia – with it numerous civil wars – was representative in Latin America, but in the twentieth century, for most countries in the region civil wars became an anachronism, and social and political experiences of incorporation were opened up under populism (Vargas in Brazil, Perón in Argentina). Yet Colombia suffered a prolonged, undeclared civil war called *la Violencia* – defined by Hobsbawm as a complex "failed revolution." Thereafter, Colombia would become increasingly exceptional within the context of Latin American politics.

Taking note of this singularity, this book is a voyage of discovery into the exceptional quality of Colombian history, which only makes sense, according to the author, in the broader context of Latin American history, and of the relations between Colombia, Western capitalism, and the United States.

According to the laws, there is only one government.
President Alberto Lleras Camargo (1945)

Introduction: Remembering Colombia

Forgetting is a key element of the system, as it is of Colombian history. It is a factor of power.

Jacques Gilard, *Veinte y cuarenta años de algo peor que la soledad* (1988)

I Setting

In late 2005, some 300 representatives from indigenous reserves (*resguardos indígenas*) and Afro-Colombian communities (*comunidades negras*) came together in Quibdó, the capital of Colombia's Chocó department, to outline strategies for survival in a war that targets them, the communities they represent, and their non-liberal, collective mode of administering resources and territory. According to the Colombian Constitution of 1991, considered one of the most progressive in the world, indigenous peoples have rights to autonomy – collective management of land and political as well as cultural self-determination through *cabildos*, cells of local government. In 1993, under Law 70, Afro-Colombians secured rights similar to those enshrined in the constitution for indigenous peoples: inalienable collective land titles managed by community councils. Both Afro-Colombians and the indigenous people built on non-liberal traditions of constituting themselves as democratic citizens and communities.

However, these collectives were threatened with extinction. As part of a protest movement, and on the basis of existing rights – conquered through processes of organizing that began in the 1970s and culminated in the Constituent Assembly of 1991 – indigenous and Afro-Colombian delegates drafted four letters that introduce the dramatis personae and outline the major themes of the current phase of Colombia's sixty-year conflict. More than a decade after their conquest of citizenship, the Chocó department still had the highest rates of poverty and infant mortality, in a country in which more than half of the population lived in poverty.[1] Communities and reserves faced dispossession at the hands of three groups: armed Left insurgencies, paramilitary counterinsurgents, and the Colombian Armed Forces and National Police – the latter backed by the US government to a fuller extent than the armed forces of any countries except Egypt, Israel, Iraq, and Afghanistan.[2]

The communities represented at the 7th Inter-Ethnic Solidarity Conference outlined a different vision of "identity, territory, culture, autonomy, and independence" than the ones held by the groups threatening their existence with "violent expropriation." From the National Liberation Army (ELN), the country's smallest insurgency, delegates asked for respect for political autonomy and territorial sovereignty: largely absent from the region, the ELN was told to stay out of indigenous reserves and black communities. Founded in the mid-1960s, and centered from the 1980s in the northern oil regions and multinational export enclave zones (coal, gold, emeralds), the ELN had between 3,500 and 4,500 combatants, and unlike most areas in which they operated, the ELN had only recently arrived in the Chocó. State and especially paramilitary repression of their narrow support base had weakened or defeated them in areas of the countryside where they had long ruled, and their urban militias were all but decimated. Hence in 2005, they began preliminary talks on peace negotiations with the right-wing administration of Álvaro Uribe Vélez.

The Revolutionary Armed Forces of Colombia (FARC) was told to stay out of deliberations in indigenous *cabildos* and Afro-Colombian community councils. Formed in the mid-1960s, the FARC has 18,000 to 22,000 combatants. By the mid-1990s, it had a presence in more than half of all county seats (*municipios*), with a stronghold in the jungles and plains in sparsely populated frontier zones of the south and southeast. By the late 1990s, the FARC and the ELN together influenced politics in over 90 per cent of frontier *municipios*. In the letter addressed to it by Chocó leaders, the FARC came in for harsh criticism:

> We reject the FARC's intrusion into our Community Councils and Indigenous Councils (*cabildos*), which compromises our

autonomy and our cultural identity; impedes the free exercise of our daily activities; serves as a pretext for the absence of the social investments that the state should make; impedes the application of internal rules and regulations; and affects our own security. You threaten and stigmatize our people with unfounded accusations that cannot be contradicted, and you create a cloak of suspicion over those who travel to and from rural zones to municipal capitals, alleging that they are Army informants. For all of these reasons, we reiterate that you must not be present either in black communities or in indigenous reserves.[3]

Insurgent attacks on and intimidation of Afro-Colombian communities and indigenous reserves – however representative of the degradation of Colombia's armed conflict – pale in comparison to the percentage of human rights violations committed by the paramilitary AUC (United Self-Defense Forces of Colombia). This climbed from roughly 65 to 80 per cent of the total during US-sponsored Plan Colombia (2000–5).

Though insurgencies depend on terrorist tactics like bombings, kidnapping, selective assassination, and extortion, little is gained in understanding by applying the "terrorist" label. To blame the bulk of the country's problems on the insurgency – fashionable academia and the media – is to put the cart before the horse. It overlooks the fact that throughout modern history, state terror has provided the "oxygen" without which insurgent terror "cannot combust for very long."[4]

Unlike Left insurgency, paramilitary dominance was intimately tied to official politics, and most evident in President Álvaro Uribe Vélez's heartland, Antioquia, as well as the Santanders, the "coffee axis" (*eje cafetero*), and the Atlantic coast region. Paramilitaries are best defined as private armies that

Collaborate with the military or undertake tasks that should be carried out by the military, such as fighting guerrillas. Or, more exactly, they take care of the dirty and disreputable aspects of this fight: the massacre of those suspected of collaborating with the guerrillas ("paraguerrillas") and the displacement of masses of the unarmed civilian population that can act as the "sea for the fish" for the guerrillas, to use the Maoist metaphor.[5]

President Uribe was reminded that after communities denounced the spread, under paramilitary auspices, of coca cultivation and narcotics trafficking in the region since 2003, the government did nothing about it other than target collectively held territories for "violent expropriation" – under the pretext of combating the drug trade. Recalling their denunciation of paramilitary and military coordination in 2004, they protested the implementation of a neoliberal agro-export model at their expense:

> The African Palm puts our collective land titles in danger, affects our fragile eco-system, damages our agriculture, affects traditional crops, creates an enclave economy, aggravates the food crisis, and implies a long process of capital accumulation that would only benefit large investors, to the detriment of our communities . . . Far from being a prosperous alternative, the African Palm represents a counter-insurgent strategy that is exacerbating the conflict in the Chocó.

The document refers to investors, capital accumulation, and extractive enclave economies – crucial aspects of Colombian integration into the US-dominated circuits of production, consumption, and distribution – the result of a shift away from coffee and protected industrial manufacturing that began in the 1970s.[6] Delegates mention a strategy of counterinsurgency which, in violation of Protocol II of the Geneva Conventions, demands loyalty and collaboration of citizens with police and armed forces, and functions to help the spread of mono-crop export agriculture with potentially ecocidal and ethnocidal effects.

The letter to President Uribe speaks to the state-sanctioned paramilitary takeover in peripheral frontier regions which the central government has never ruled, and where oil, banana, gold, and logging companies functioned as a resource base – a necessary condition for insurgent expansion and consolidation. In keeping with a precedent set during *la Violencia* in the 1950s, President Uribe began to institutionalize parastate impunity in order to strengthen central government authority over frontier zones – a dangerous repetition of the past. Violent dispossession was comparable to the earlier period in the 1950s, with 3 million displaced in the twenty-first century, mainly in multinational export enclaves or areas of recent frontier settlement. For the most part, this is carried out in the name of fighting the "internal enemy."[7]

Although political party elites no longer led the process, right-wing paramilitaries – and, to a lesser extent, Left guerrilla insurgencies – continue to forcibly displace peasants from the land.[8] Delegates to the Inter-Ethnic Solidarity Conference therefore demanded an end to impunity, expropriation, and displacement, as well as reparations for crimes committed against their communities. While expressing support for a plan for reintegration of former paramilitary combatants into civilian life, the letter to President Uribe warned that paramilitary demobilization could give rise to "new paramilitary structures," and asked for "disarmament, demobilization, and reintegration into civilian life . . . within a framework of respect for truth, justice, reparations, and non-repetition." In honor of their "autonomy," they asked that "re-insertion not become a mechanism for the expropriation of our ancestral lands."

The emphasis on memory, truth, justice, reparations, and expropriation was a response to President Uribe's Law 975 on paramilitary demobilization, which offered none of the above.[9] As Human Rights Watch emphasized, the law did nothing to dismantle paramilitary power and "flagrantly violated" international norms on issues of truth, justice, and reparations to victims and their families.[10] With its long Pacific shoreline, thick jungle, dense web of rivers, and mountainous border with Panama, the Chocó became a strategic corridor (*corredor estratégico*) for the counterinsurgency, which – for the time being, anyway – has defeated the FARC. Both insurgency and counterinsurgency forced Afro-Colombian and indigenous communities to pay taxes and tribute, and fought to use their territory for coca growing, cocaine processing and transport, and arms trafficking.

The second group, it bears repeating, worked with the Colombian military, infiltrated official institutions, "demobilized" under a law that regulated their impunity, and became a parastate – a state within and alongside the official state. At least in theory, insurgents, however, fought to overthrow the Colombian state, and controlled over 40 per cent of national territory. The more the US government has backed the Colombian Armed Forces and National Police against the insurgencies, the more powerful the right-wing parastate has become. This, then, is one of the unintended consequences of a counterinsurgent policy to strengthen a weak state.

The Colombian war has created the second-largest internally displaced population in the world after Sudan, with Afro-Colombians comprising the majority of the displaced; indigenous peoples represented a disproportionately high percentage as well.[11] The region's third-largest country, Colombia had the second-largest population of African descent in Latin America.

Patterns of expropriation there reflect long-term historical continuities in landownership, exploitation of natural resources, and the use of political terror in a parliamentary democratic republic founded upon unresolved legacies of conquest, colonization, and slavery.[12] Under Spanish colonialism, for example, African slaves were brought from Cartagena, the chief slave port of the Andean region, to work in gold mines and on cattle ranches in the Chocó, which led to the displacement or dispossession of indigenous groups. Seeking freedom from an extractive enclave economy and extensive, absentee-owned *latifundios*, the indigenous, like manumitted slaves and runaways, fled into jungles that are today the eye of the hurricane.[13]

The Inter-Ethnic Solidarity Forum called on all parties to search for a negotiated political, as opposed to military, solution to the war, outlining a different vision of peace, security, democracy, justice – and, not least, truth – than those on offer from the state, the right-wing parastate, and the Left insurgencies. Communally based forms of nonliberal democracy and citizenship, linked to a new Left electoral movement, offer a way forward, but because of the violent exclusiveness of both the political system and the reigning neoliberal economic model, the way is blocked.

II Aim

Although Colombia's civil war is one of the longest-running and most violent, its historical depth is rarely acknowledged. Considered the least understood and least studied of Latin American countries in the USA, it earned its place on the map of counterinsurgency planners in the new imperial landscape of the twenty-first century.[14] Given Colombia's geographic proximity to the USA, as well as the length and depth of US military engagement there, the relative silence in English-language scholarship and public debate is unsettling.

In what follows, I build almost entirely on the work of scholars, particularly historians and social scientists, as well as journalists and human rights workers, in order to connect, as well as untangle, past and present.[15] Literature on the contemporary period typically contains a chapter on the history of political violence in Colombia, but a deeper historical perspective is needed to understand the current moment. Existing historical syntheses, however, give short shrift to radical-popular movements, emphasizing instead actions of elite groups, the two political parties they dominated, and the rise of the nation state.

This book attempts to remedy this problem in the literature. In proportion to the progressive hypertrophy of armed Left insurgencies, it is true, radical-popular mobilization in Colombia has been comparatively weak and fragmented since the 1960s, but it was not always so. Radical-popular movements have punctuated Colombian history at specific conjunctures, with lasting effects, and an understanding of their history gives us a more rounded view of nation state, party, and ruling-class formation. It also helps to explain Colombia's extraordinarily high levels of political violence, which set it on a different, bloodier course from neighbors during the cold war – Latin America's darkest era of political terror since conquest. While radical popular movements and social democratic electoral parties came to power throughout Latin America in the early twenty-first century, in Colombia there was a "progressive invasion of more and more public and private spaces" by a violence that had become "the ordering-disordering factor of politics, society, and the economy."[16]

The central claim of this book is that to understand the Colombian civil war today, it is necessary to appreciate the multiple layers of previous conflicts and the accumulated weight of unresolved contradictions.[17] Past and present "illuminate each other reciprocally," and signal the danger, in the Colombian case, of repeating collective political trauma.[18] Contemporary conflict in Colombia mirrors the past, with major transfers of property and territory to the wealthy and powerful, as well as another round of official amnesia regarding war crimes – legislated in the name of "peace" and "national reconciliation." I situate current debates on memory, truth, justice, and reparations in light of what has come before. As one scholar of state terror in Latin America reminds us, "recovery begins with memory,', and this book is offered as part of the struggle against forgetting.[19] One effect of the long-term use of political terror in Colombia and elsewhere has been to erase the memory of the political alternatives to which terror responded.

III Themes

In policy-making circles in Washington and Bogotá, it is often argued that Colombia suffers from a culture of violence, as if Colombians had an innate propensity to shed one another's blood.[20] As commonly presented, this is an ahistorical and tautological explanation of why, in contrast to neighbors characterized by center-Left governments and popular mobilization, Colombian politics are characterized by high levels of terror. And it overlooks the fact that until the end of the nineteenth century, Colombia, in contrast to Brazil, Mexico, Chile, and Argentina, was marked "not by its mass violence, but by the lack thereof."[21] Whether focusing on comparisons with other countries in the region or on the difference between the nineteenth and twentieth centuries, scholars generally caution against interpreting late twentieth-century violence as a logical outcome of nineteenth-century patterns. There is scant historical evidence to support the idea that a "culture of violence" explains Colombian politics.

In explaining Colombia's unusual path, two classic accounts of comparative Latin American history stress the durability of oligarchic democracy, institutionalized through two political parties.[22] More recently, the idea of an "oligarchy" has been subject to skeptical critique, yet remains useful for understanding Colombia's violence in relation to an exclusionary political order.[23] We can understand the oligarchy as a quasi-corporate group, most of whose members enjoy privileges based on birth and something like rank, supplemented by the entrance of new elements, mainly from the middle class, but occasionally from the working class and peasantry. With presidential elections held like clockwork every four years, Colombia's oligarchic democracy boasts the longest-running two-party system in the world. The Conservative-Liberal diarchy survived nearly 150 years, remaining outwardly intact down to the twenty-first century, despite legislative elections governed by proportional representation.

After 1848, when Liberal and Conservative rule was established, no fraction of the oligarchy united the class as a whole, along with subordinate groups, in a hegemonic project; none could represent its interests as those of the nation. Though this was common in Europe and Latin America in the nineteenth century, in Colombia it lasted through the twenty-first century. Elites were therefore forced to enter into political pacts with subordinate groups that did not enact public rituals of deference, let alone internalize the norms and values of their rulers.[24] Instead, they demanded and fought for equality; but in lieu of bourgeois capitalist hegemony, authoritarian Catholic clientelism, underwritten by the rise of coffee export capitalism and the Conservative Party, dominated the fifty-year period after 1880, and reversed the tide of radical-popular mobilization that had characterized Colombia during the "Age of Capital" (1848–75).

Revanchism and increasing technological sophistication complemented each other during the coffee export boom, Colombia's own age of capital, which did not lead to an extension of central government authority, but strengthened the two political parties through which geographically fragmented, landed oligarchies maintained regional and local supremacy in the face of challenges from below. I argue that the short reach of the central government, the influence of the two parties, pronounced regionalism based on landownership, and ruling-class disunity have been constants in republican history.

As the coffee frontier was settled in the late nineteenth and early twentieth centuries, sectors of the peasantry identified with whiteness and capitalist progress secured property rights and political incorporation into one of the two parties through networks of patronage and clientelism.[25] The majority of peasants, as well as Afro-Colombian and indigenous reserves, had precarious claims to property rights, limited incorporation into the two parties, and lived under threat of violence and/or dispossession. When reforms from above coincided with mobilization from below in the 1860s, and again in the 1930s, landlords launched reactions in the countryside, mobilizing clients to protect racial-ethnic privileges, political monopoly, and the rule of property. These movements of counter-reform, like the radical-popular movements to which they responded, were locally and regionally organized. This reflected the nature of landed wealth, political power, and authority in Colombia – fractured and mostly rural through the 1950s.

The contrast between Colombia and the rest of Latin America in the 1930s and 1940s could not be sharper: Mexico under Cárdenas, Argentina under Perón, Brazil under Vargas, Bolivia under Toro and Busch, or, as recent scholarship has shown, Cuba under Batista, the Dominican Republic under Trujillo, or Nicaragua under Somoza.[26] A form of politics that included those excluded from the oligarchic republics in order to forestall real or imagined threats of revolution, populism succeeded brilliantly. While the middle class and fractions of the old oligarchies may have benefited more than other groups, the working class and peasantry benefited more than they had before, or since.

In Colombia, however, populism was beaten back in the 1930s and 1940s. When it reared its head again in the 1970s and 1980s, it was decapitated by state and parastate terror. Ironically, this has only weakened the already fragile legitimacy of the central government, and strengthened, at least militarily and territorially, Left insurgencies and the right-wing counterinsurgency. By scholarly consensus, this makes Colombia unique.[27] I argue that when the central government attempted agrarian reform under the pressure of radical-popular mobilization, reform was blocked and counter-reform strengthened in regions and municipalities. As sectarian warfare spread in the 1940s and 1950s, hundreds of thousands of displaced peasant families either colonized agrarian frontiers in sparsely populated lowland regions, or carved out urban frontiers ringing Colombia's numerous intermediate cities, in zones far from the radius of central government authority.

First through factional warfare between two parties, and later through cold war counterinsurgency, the central government delegated repression when faced with insurgent challenges. This was common in the counter-insurgent terror states that began with Guatemala in 1954, Brazil and Bolivia in 1964, and spread through the Southern Cone in the 1970s. As elsewhere after the Second World War, US government patrons were "distant yet still involved" in Latin America, and "counterrevolutionary terror was inextricably tied to empire."[28]

Two things made Colombia's terror state distinctive, though: first, part of the peasantry, linked to elites through middle-class intermediaries and the dream of property ownership, drove others off the land through terror, dispossession, and expropriation – roughly analogous to what Marx called the "primitive accumulation" of capital in the English countryside.[29] Second, over time, the paramilitaries obtained relative autonomy from the state by becoming a parastate. This concentrated land in fewer and fewer hands, even as it redistributed a small amount of it among a select number of subaltern clients.[30] Cities grew alongside the settlement of an open agrarian frontier, where the previous dynamic of conflict was replicated.[31] And Colombians, in the course of just fifty years, went from living in a society in which two-thirds of people lived on the land – *patrón* and *campesino; criollo*, mestizo, *mulato, indio* and *negro* – to one in which two-thirds lived in cities.

Even as Colombia has become a society that revolves around a network of cities connected by air and highways, landlords have retained political traction in regions and localities. Colombian politics can be envisioned as an authoritarian parliamentary system in which landlords, rather than coming into conflict with rising merchant-industrial groups, have fused with them.[32] Commercial activity, characterized by an unclear division between licit and illicit, has continuously provided the oligarchy with outsiders and fresh initiatives, as upwardly mobile sectors sought – and found – entry into the ranks of the oligarchy through ruthless entrepreneurialism.[33]

New manufacturing and commercial elites tied to the coffee export business joined with the landed oligarchy in the late nineteenth century, and rather than weakening the power of the landlordism within the oligarchy, this strengthened it. The reactionary alliance characterized the coffee republic under Conservative rule after 1880, survived intact the *gaitanista* challenge in the 1940s, provided the basis for National Front policies through the 1980s, and, thanks to the US government's "war on drugs," took on new dimensions with the continued rise of the cocaine business in the 1990s. The drug export mafia invested in construction, communication, and services, and its contraband imports undercut domestic manufacturing industry. As *latifundistas*, they owned most of the country's best land and urban real estate. Based on landownership, power continued to be dispersed from a weak center into the regions, especially in frontier areas, beyond the reach of the state.

The "chronic deficit" of the Colombian state is proverbial among scholars and those living through the conflict. Specialists and social actors with conflicting views of Colombian politics agree that the Colombian state is weak, its authority brittle. In any account of Colombia's violence, this must rank as a principal explanatory factor for the strength of insurgencies and the paramilitaries. Sovereignty has always been region-ally circumscribed and fragmented. The central government has never monopolized force legitimately, nor has it administered the majority of the territory under its jurisdiction. This led to a long period of inter-elite factional conflict that spilled into civil war through the first half of the twentieth century.

By the end of the 1950s, however, the bipartisan grip on formal political representation was backed by a shared commitment to liberal market economics, in which the state was to play a limited role. Cold war anti-communism cemented the two parties together in the National Front. Wealth, especially land, remained tightly concentrated, its distribution highly unequal, although a period of sustained economic growth – based on coffee exports and manufacturing for the home market – broadened the urban and small-town middle class in cities and *municipios*. Elite consensus without hegemony absorbed segments of subordinate groups through networks of patronage and clientelism. A modest middle class, as well as subaltern clients from the peasantry and working class, were increasingly tied to this new order. But by criminalizing protest, dissent, and the very poverty that government economic policies reproduced, the National Front excluded the majority in town and country.

National Front counterinsurgency spurred the growth of Left insurgencies. In the 1970s and 1980s, recently colonized rural and urban areas without state presence became fertile terrain for national-level, cross-class, multi-ethnic Left electoral movements. Since these were led by Left insurgents looking to open up the political system or overthrow it, landlord militias – backed by a new ruling-class faction of cocaine entrepreneurs – fought to protect private property rights against "subversive" threats by liquidating the broad Left.

Created as an auxiliary to the state's military and police forces, who were unable to stop the spread of insurgency, paramilitaries were poised to become the new rulers of the land by the beginning of the twenty-first century. Theirs was a "gangsterism that had become society itself."[34] Paramilitaries evolved into a parastate, penetrating political parties as well as government agencies, from the Constitutional Court to intelligence services nominally under presidential control. In many regions, paramilitaries administered territory and monopolized public office. Insurgencies functioned as tributary statelets, charging taxes and protection rents on the cocaine business, multinational extractive enterprises, and landlords, as well as the inhabitants of their "zones." Regimes of "parcellized sovereignty" and "fragmented peace" led to an international humanitarian crisis that overran national borders and threatened the sovereignty of neighboring states.[35] These, then, are the outlines of the history and politics of a country that has become the principal ally of the US government – and chief recipient of US military aid – in the western hemisphere.

1

Radical-Popular Republicanism, 1848–80

We should be treated like citizens of a republic and not like the slaves of a sultan.

Afro-Colombian boatmen from Dagua (1851)

This chapter introduces the economic, demographic, and political outlines of early republican Colombia, and analyzes the social history of politics. In spite of features of oligarchic rule it shared with neighboring republics following the wars of independence, in the "Age of Capital" (1848–75), radical-popular political mobilization put Colombia at the leading edge of Atlantic republican democracies.[36] A closer look at the Cauca, one of Colombia's key regions in the nineteenth century, demonstrates that, contrary to what scholars have commonly assumed, oppressed racial/ethnic groups and classes fought to claim places in the new republic. They forged political traditions that challenged slavery and ongoing processes of conquest. A closer look at these traditions moves us away from static, ahistorical images of a united, all-powerful landed oligarchy, ruling over a hapless, dependent peasantry, revealing more complex local and regional dynamics. In contrast to the long period of reaction that followed it, as well as in comparison to its neighbors at the time, Colombia was notable for its radical-popular politics.

I From the Top Down

Colombia emerged from the wars of independence one of the most devastated, disunited, and economically depressed of new Latin American nations, with miserable communications, little foreign trade, no banking institutions, and low fiscal capacity. Public works were non-existent, and the internal market was tiny: as late as 1890, it cost more to transport coffee from Medellín to Bogotá than from Medellín to London.[37] In the 1850s and 1860s, brief export booms in quinine and tobacco, the latter of which peaked during the US Civil War, did not lead to socioeconomic transformation, and the penury of Bogotá's unproductive, overconsuming aristocracy was the subject of nostalgic lament.[38] With credit scarce, Antioquian merchant-lenders – grown rich off profits from gold mining in the late colonial and early republican periods – acted as financiers, but did not try to unite other ruling fractions behind them. In 1854, they even made noises about separating from Colombia to become part of the USA.[39]

Extreme geographical differentiation has always been an inescapable factor of Colombian politics, and has allowed elites to entrench their power in land, political office, and market share at the local and regional levels. The country is rent by three great mountain ranges fanning up from the south, themselves split by the Cauca and Magdalena rivers. To the southeast, it opens out onto a vast expanse of tropical lowlands, straddling the equator, crisscrossed by innumerable rivers draining into the Orinoco and Amazon basins. To the west and north lie the Caribbean and Pacific coasts, and the impenetrable jungle of the Panamanian Isthmus, while the country's principal oil reserves lie in the easterly province of Arauca and Northern Santander, fronting the Venezuelan border. The majority of the population has always been concentrated in the cooler, subtropical mountainous regions. Bogotá, at 8,660 feet above sea level, has an average temperature of 57 °F (14 °C). But the cities themselves were, for centuries, separated by tortuous roads and impassable mountains, as they remain for peasants in frontier areas.

Poor transport and geographical isolation have had a critical shaping effect on the ruling groups themselves. Centralized military control was inherently more difficult in Colombia than in neighboring countries: relative to population, the army was always about a third of the size of that in Peru or Ecuador.[40] Civilian parties – and the Church – thus became much more important as transmission belts of power than elsewhere. But they could not escape the logic of territorial fragmentation either. By delegating authority to local party bosses, Bogotá's landlord-merchant-lawyers helped intensify, rather than mitigate, regional divisions and inequalities. Citizenship in late nineteenth- and early twentieth-century Colombia did not entail a sense of common belonging within the nation, represented by a central government, but rather an exclusive membership in one of two political parties. Politics, defined in terms of friend-enemy, was a zero-sum affair in the regions and municipalities, and party affiliations cut across racial, class, ethnic, and regional lines.[41]

While the two parties have often shed each other's blood, the classic political paradigm – structured, along Iberian lines, by an oligarchic division between Conservatives and Liberals – has persisted. The system was characteristic of the newly independent Latin American states of the early nineteenth century, where a ruling elite of landowners, lawyers, and merchants, manipulating a restricted suffrage in which those who had the vote were clients rather than citizens, typically split into two wings. Conservatives were devoted first and foremost to order, and – like their counterparts in Europe – religion, in close alliance with the Catholic Church. Liberals declared themselves in favor of progress, and were, on the whole, anticlerical. Economically speaking, landed wealth tended to be more Conservative, commercial fortunes more Liberal, although occupational differences were not particularly pronounced, much less decisive. Aside from Liberal anticlericalism, there were no major ideological fault lines either. The civilian division, almost purely sectarian, was punctuated by *pronunciamientos* and seizures of power by rival military chieftains, in the name – but not always with the assent – of one or other of the opposing political parties.

Although the country was divided between two great political loyalties, these showed no systematic regional pattern. A few zones did exhibit a clear-cut predominance of one or other party early on: the Caribbean littoral was Liberal; Antioquia was Conservative. But these were the exceptions.[42] The rule was an intricate quilt of local rivalries at the micro-level of small communities or townships, cheek by jowl within each region. Liberals and Conservatives were, from the start, and have remained, highly factional as nationwide organizations.

Originally, the division between Liberals and Conservatives had a rational ideological foundation in Colombian society. Liberals were lay-minded members of the landed and merchant elite, followers of Santander, and hostile to what was perceived as the clerical and militarist compromises of the last period of Bolívar's career as Liberator. Conservatives, who had closer links to the colonial aristocracy or officialdom, stood for centralized order and the social discipline of religion. Ideas mattered in disputes between the two, starting with the Santander government's directive that Bentham's treatises on civil and penal legislation be mandatory study in the University of Bogotá, as early as 1825 – inconceivable in England itself even fifty years later. Furious clerical reaction eventually led to the reintroduction of the Jesuits, who had been expelled from the colonies by the Spanish monarchy in 1767, to run the secondary schools; and then their re-expulsion in 1850.[43]

II From the Bottom Up

Colombia was at the forefront of liberal revolution in the nineteenth-century Atlantic world, and Liberal Party leaders, confident of their historical mission, were committed to radical reforms. Slavery and the death penalty were to be abolished, Church and state separated, clerical quit-rents lifted, divorce legalized, the army reduced, and universal male suffrage introduced. In its view, Indian communities, seen as part of a pernicious colonial legacy to be overcome, had no place in the republic, which was to be founded instead on yeoman smallholders. This had been the vision of Bolívar.

In the Cauca, Afro-Colombians, Indians, and frontier settlers from Antioquia pressed claims and participated actively in politics. A political culture of "republican bargaining" developed after 1848. Subalterns voted in elections, and participated in town councils, democratic societies, demonstrations, boycotts, riots, and civil wars, making Colombia one of the world's most participatory republican democracies during the "Age of Capital" (1848–76). Nowhere else in the Atlantic world of the 1850s and early 1860s did descendants of African slaves vote and join *Sociedades Democráticas*, and nowhere else did Indian community members exercise the vote as citizens.

In the 1850s, no ruling faction was powerful enough to implant regional, let alone national, hegemony in Colombia. Each clique that aspired to state power had, to varying extents, to forge local- and regional-level alliances with previously disenfranchised groups, whose demands included the end of inequalities that stemmed from patterns of colonial domination and exploitation. Cauca's elites had to contend with artisans and rural worker-citizen-soldiers: Indians, Afro-Caucanos, and Antioquian frontier settlers. Rulers and ruled in Colombia did not have a shared understanding of republican democracy, nor a joint commitment to equality. Conservatives and many elite Liberals thought democracy should not give way to a leveling process and a "republic of equals" in which "anarchy" reigned, whereas for Afro-Caucanos, equality meant the end of slavery and the rule of Conservative *hacendados*, as well as access to land of their own. For Indians in the Cauca, equality meant the right to exist as a corporate group exercising collective stewardship of land and practicing village self-government. In the north, for Antioquian settler villages, equality meant protection from Conservative merchant-land speculators from back home.

The clash between Liberals and Conservatives, then, was not just over questions of education, nor was it a purely intra-elite affair: the Liberal Revolution of 1849–53 was preceded and deepened by risings (*zurriagos*) of mostly Afro-ex-slave insurgents against Conservative *hacendados* in the Cauca Valley, with looting, arson, fence-smashing, and land occupations widespread after 1850. The leading Conservative clan's hacienda, Japio, was occupied at the end of the war in 1851, as Afro-Caucanos practiced communal landholding and collective use of forests and rivers. They sought to produce and market tobacco and sugar, free from the rule of *hacendados*. Radical republican artisans in the capital, Bogotá, stirred by the Parisian barricades of 1848 and the writings of Proudhon and Louis Blanc, mobilized as well. As in Europe, Colombian Liberals abandoned their craftsmen supporters to the rigors of free trade, and began to dissolve communally held indigenous lands. They did not dispense with their Afro-Caucano allies, fomenting instead the spread of *Sociedades Democráticas*, which oversaw the performance of elected officials, and petitioned local and national government authorities on issues such as primary education, voting rights, pensions, land distribution, access to the commons, and aguardiente taxes.

Liberal divisions, brought on by racial fear and rejection of insurgent Afro-Caucano Liberals, led to a Conservative upsurge in the elections of 1853, as Conservatives forged an ephemeral alliance with Indians opposed to the privatization of common lands for the benefit of speculators hungry for cinchona bark (quinine). In 1854, José María Melo led a Liberal rising that found support among Bogotá's radical republican artisans, but which caused many elite Liberals to throw their weight behind Conservatives. In Cauca, Conservatives, redefining the civil war as an outbreak of criminal banditry, took revenge on the newly minted Afro-Caucano worker-soldier-citizens by tightening vagrancy laws, reinstating the death penalty, and trying to ban the *Sociedades Democráticas*. Though suffrage rights were not abolished, the goal was to disenfranchise ex-slaves, and a variety of means, including terror, were employed to keep Afro-Caucanos from voting. Liberals paid dearly for their underestimation of the weight of the Indian communities, but Conservatives were not astute enough to design a counterpart to the *Sociedades Democráticas* in order to cement an alliance with Indian *resguardos*.

In the late 1850s, Tomás Cipriano de Mosquera, leader of the Cauca's Conservatives before 1848, and a descendant of "the royal family of New Granada," led the Liberal insurgency. Along with the Conservative Arboleda clan, to which they had close ties, the Mosqueras were the largest landholders in the region. Mosquera fought under Bolívar, and occupied important posts under proto-Conservative governments, but in his bid to oust Mariano Ospina, he defected to the Liberal side and looked for allies among Afro-Caucanos, Indians, and Antioquian settlers. Liberals sought to repeal the hated vagrancy laws, the death penalty, and stop the onslaught on the Indian *resguardos*. They recognized village self-government through Law 90 in 1859, and protected Antioquian settlers in María from Conservative speculators – with whom Conservative Ospina had personal connections – in the mountainous Quindío, blocking hated consumption taxes on liquor as well.

As Conservatives failed to craft durable alliances with Indian communities, Liberals capitalized on their mass following among Afro-Caucanos to defeat their rivals in a civil war (1860–63), in which, according to one Conservative, Mosquera's troops were "composed of blacks, zambos, and mulattos, assassins and thieves of the Cauca valley."[44] The dark-skinned popular forces fought under Mosquera, although of the indigenous groups, only the Páez (Nasa) openly sided with Liberals; Conservatives alienated former Indian allies by conscripting adult men and hanging those who resisted. They counted on a thin base of support from mestizo smallholders and some Antioquian villages.

Once Mosquera became president in 1863, Cauca became the country's leading region, as Mosquera devolved suffrage rights to the states (thus re-enfranchising Afro-Caucanos), sequestered Church lands, radically decentralized the constitution, abolished vagrancy laws and the death penalty, and recognized Indian *resguardos* as well as settler claims. Judges and deputies in the state legislature, as well as state presidents, were elected every two years, as were municipal councils. Voting took place throughout the year. Liberals controlled the outcomes of state elections, but Conservatives won seats in the state legislature and competed in local elections.

The combination of a barrage of Liberal policies, electoral supremacy, and the irruption of participatory, radical-popular democracy within the Liberal Party, forced a more intransigent clerical and internally colonial Conservatism into being. With the divide between elite Liberals and their subaltern allies widening along racial and class lines, and clashes growing over the meanings of republican democracy growing through the late 1870s, the limits of the alliance had been reached.

III   Tropical Thermidor

Elite Liberals were not willing to dismantle the hacienda, which would have radically reconfigured political power based on the ownership of land and exploitation of slave labor. Determined to stop the swelling tide of what they called "anarchy" under radical Liberals – private property was under attack; bandits and rustlers loomed in nearby mountains; tenants and sharecroppers refused to work or pay rent – elite Liberals known as the Independents broke ranks. The holy trinity was "family, property, and religion." Independents had support from formerly Liberal Antioquian settlers in María, as well as "white" and "mestizo" small-holders in northern Cauca, while Indian communities remained neutral.

This allowed Conservatives to lead a bloody but successful religious coup in the Cauca in 1878–79, which brought an end to Cauca's, and Colombia's, radical-popular republican experiment.[45] Conservatives, opposed to what they called "savage democracy," in which "the barbarous element predominated," eagerly backed Independents, and were determined to roll back as many of the new changes as they could. In the 1870s, they founded a political vehicle – Catholic Societies – through which they enlisted the support of frontier smallholders, some of them former Liberals, for such a project. By providing religious education, Catholic Societies aggressively combated anticlerical Liberal educational reforms. Revamped Conservatism, pioneered by Caucano Independents and popular republican smallholders, led to the backlash known as the Regeneration under Rafael Núñez.

This view of the history of ethnic/racial and class conflict reveals that in any search for a more peaceful, democratic, and equitable future, Colombians can look back to a political culture that featured ample channels for subaltern participation, from the 1850s through the 1870s. It shows that the spread of authoritarian clientelism that characterized the end of the period evolved as a reaction against the threat to private property, racial privilege, and political monopoly. The Regeneration – the subject of the next chapter – affected political life in the twentieth century so profoundly that it is often forgotten how vital the democratic tendencies that preceded it had been.

2

From Reaction to Rebellion, 1880–1930

Three distinct races . . . form the population of the republic. Each
state has diverse climates, customs, and labors. There are only two
links that unite: language and religion. They have not been able to
take language from us but they try to uproot our beliefs. Barbar-
ians! . . . They threw God and law out of government and higher
education, and now you will be the result: if we are not already
irremediably ruined, it is because Christ still reigns in hearts and
minds.

Monseñor Rafael María Carrasquilla (1885)

The implementation of an authoritarian centralist project overseen by
the Catholic Church and the Conservative Party marked the fifty-year
period after 1880. It proscribed radical-popular politics by strengthening
a clientelism rooted in the coffee export boom, which began in the 1880s
and brought the Conservative commercial and banking elites of Antioquia to national prominence. This group of entrepreneurs paid for and
benefited from the settlement of the coffee frontier, which offered hope
of landownership to tenants and sharecroppers willing to migrate. The
idealized figure of Conservative Antioquia, symbolized by the light-
skinned, property-owning frontier settler, became the measure of national progress, in contrast to the dark-skinned tenant, sharecropper, or
communal landholder in the Cauca.[46]

I Coffee Capitalism and Clientelism

Begun in 1880, the Regeneration initiated five decades of reaction,
dashing the hopes of Liberals who wished to see Colombia stand

alongside leading Atlantic democracies. For the most part, "Colombia's elites turned away from trying to incorporate a disciplined citizenry, instead focusing their efforts on ruling over recalcitrant subjects."[47] The constitution of 1886 strengthened the power of the center, giving the president the authority to appoint provincial governors, and terms of office were extended from two to six years for the executive, and from two to four years for the legislative, to reduce the frequency of elections. Demonstrations were forbidden, *Sociedades Democráticas* persecuted, and "order" became the watchword of the day. The country was "ideologically imprisoned," and Catholic, Hispanofile grammarians like Miguel Antonio Caro – the architect of the 1886 Constitution – were its guardians.[48]

Subalterns were forced to work for and obey creoles, and the sphere of politics was reduced to exclude them. A professional army replaced popular militias, and the death penalty was reinstated to halt attacks on property. The new concordat with the Vatican ensured a tight link with the most authoritarian currents of the Church, which dispatched successive waves of battle-hardened zealots from other theatres of struggle – European or Latin American – to fortify the faith in Colombia and run the public school system. At the end of the century, the Regeneration regime crushed Liberal resistance, associated with the rising coffee bourgeoisie, in the murderous War of a Thousand Days (1899–1903), which left 100,000 dead. President Marco Fidel Suárez, a mestizo from an Antioquian peasant family who joined the elite, jettisoned Panama to the USA, whose dominance of hemispheric affairs went uncontested thereafter (except from below).[49]

The Regeneration cemented oligarchic control – not seriously threatened during the War of a Thousand Days – and closed off avenues for radical-popular democratic participation that a heterogeneous coalition of rural workers, provincial middle-class lawyers (*tinterillos*), and urban artisans opened up after mid-century.[50] Indians, artisans, and Afro-Colombians saw citizenship rights restricted under Conservatives, and the Catholic *raza antioqueña*, mythologized in the image of the small-holding Antioquian settler, became the cultural linchpin of the new political-economic order.

Núñez's authoritarian, anti-democratic road was paved over the bodies of those who struggled for alternative, more inclusive participatory republican projects. It set the parameters for national politics down to the twenty-first century. The reasons for such persistence have evidently had to do with topography: since the onset of the Regeneration, Colombia's geographical configuration has awarded Liberal-Conservative elites an exceptional logistical advantage in imposing parochial clientelist controls from above, while blocking or suppressing nationwide mobilizations from below. After elite Liberals had run up against their own contradictions in the 1870s, what the parties lost in horizontal cohesion, they gained in vertical grip on their followers. The intense material and ideological forces of their mutual contention were applied in intimate grass-roots settings; the exceptional strength of the clientelism established during the Regeneration no doubt owes much to the particular localization of these pressures.

Another feature of the Colombian countryside both reinforced this clientelism and gave it an unusual political twist. It was the discovery, from the 1870s, that large parts of its highland frontiers were ideal terrain for the cultivation of coffee that gave Colombian merchants a major export staple, generating substantial earnings and the prospect of capitalist transformation. Starting in Santander as an extension of Venezuelan coffee farms, peasant settlers planted westwards into Cundinamarca, and, by the end of the century, Tolima, Antioquia, and Viejo Caldas (Caldas, Risaralda, Quindío). After the First World War, Colombia had become the world's second-largest producer after Brazil, but the pattern of its coffee economy was distinctive. In Brazil and Guatemala, large plantations worked by indebted peasants or seasonal wage-laborers predominated. In Colombia such estates were more modest, peaked earlier, as in Santander, and had less weight in the overall pattern of cultivation, while medium or smallholdings were increasingly numerous, if not to the same extent as in Costa Rica. Compared with the great *fazendas* of São Paulo, however, the social base of coffee agriculture in Antioquia, Viejo Caldas, and parts of Tolima – if still highly unequal – offered tenants and sharecroppers hope of ownership and control of production. Measured in terms of land distribution, the coffee export economy was comparatively democratic. With important regional exceptions, such as Cundinamarca and eastern Tolima, production was controlled not by planters, but by peasant families working on small and medium-sized plots at mid-level altitudes, between 1,000 and 2,000 meters.

The commercialization of the crop, however, was always in the hands of a wealthy elite, anchored in Antioquia after the 1890s. They advanced credit to small farmers, tenants, and sharecroppers, purchased output, and financed its export.[51] Small producers were thus often thrust into conflict with merchant-creditors and real-estate speculators over land titles, terms of sale for their crop, and contraband trade in liquor. Even on large estates in Cundinamarca, landlord-merchants, like the *hacendados* in the Cauca before them, had to contend with fractious tenants who poached, smuggled, squatted, dealt in moonshine, and rioted over tax hikes.[52] Profit margins depended on the maintenance of an oligarchic monopoly, in the market as much as in party politics, but the powerful, landed, and well connected were far from all-powerful.[53] Nevertheless, in the coffee axis of the western highlands, the general interconnection between smallholdings below and powerful distributors above distinguished relations of production and exchange during the period of Conservative rule. It reproduced colonial ties of dependence in new forms, reinforcing vertical clientelist bonds, and idealized the hardworking, deferential yet independent – and most importantly, neither black nor Indian – coffee settler. Elsewhere in Latin America, this pattern had given way to a largely urban-based politics, in which radical populist parties – forging cross-class coalitions composed of organized labor, expanding middle sectors, and mobilized peasants – called for structural changes in the organization of the state, society, and the economy.

II Antioquian Ascendancy

The richest and most powerful of all coffee regions in Colombia was Antioquia, whose elite was distinguished by allegiance to the Church, a cult of "order," fetishization of capitalist "progress," a devotion to white supremacy, and shared commitment to a bipartisan, technocratic governance that excluded religiously intra-class sectarianism. The rise of Conservative forces of "order and progress" – during a period of scientific racist retrenchment in the Black Atlantic world (the US South, Brazil, Cuba), and ethnocidal liberalism in Meso-America and the Andes – had its economic foundation in the coffee export boom. Control of coffee – particularly transport, credit, and distribution – helped the merchant bankers of Medellín become the country's leading industrial manufacturers. *Paisa* (Antioquian) elites enjoyed national political pre-eminence from 1910 until 1930.

The movement of settlers onto coffee frontiers in the central and western highlands – generally regarded as the major historical transformation of the Conservative period – did not lead to greater equality of access to wealth, resources, or political power, though it brought smallholders into alignment with elites of one of the two parties.[53] The coffee export boom also drove the development of modern banking and credit institutions, the growth of manufacturing industry – beverages, textiles, food processing, glass, and iron works – initially based on migrant women's labor, and the construction of new transport infrastructure.[54] Rail connections linked Medellín to Puerto Berrío and the Magdalena River in 1914, and Cali to Buenaventura and the Pacific in 1915, making Valle del Cauca and its modernized sugar industry a rival pole of capitalist development.

To boost coffee exports and industrial production for the home market, the Conservative government, supported by the opposition Liberal Party, sponsored public works and education for the first time. Engineering, institutionalized in Medellín's *Escuela de Minas* after 1888, produced future presidents (Pedro Nel Ospina, Mariano Ospina Pérez, Laureano Gómez) and guided implementation of technocratic projects. Modeled after UC Berkeley's School of Mines, the *Escuela de Minas* was the seedbed of socialization for leading cadres of the new order. The school helped form a technocratic business elite – with little invested in experimental natural or social sciences, much less the arts – that thrived in the deep freeze of the Regeneration. The doctrines of Pope Leon XIII reconciled applied scientific positivism with traditionalist faith.[55]

These developments were coeval with scientific racist discourses and practices of internal colonialism vis-à-vis indigenous, mixed-race, and Afro-Colombians on the regional periphery and the coffee axis itself. In sharp contrast to the Caucano elites that had split over the relationship to Afro-Colombians, *paisa* rulers successfully integrated elements of popular culture into an internally coherent, hegemonic racial-regional ideology of whiteness and entrepreneurial wherewithal – a tropical Yankeeism.[56] Antioquian merchants benefited from extraction of natural resources like gold and oil, developed extensive cattle ranches designed to feed a burgeoning urban population, which quintupled between 1912 and 1951, and fostered a national culture of commercial coffee smallholding. Given that US corporations controlled bananas, gold, and petroleum, the fortunes of *paisa* merchant-banker-industrialists hinged on control of coffee, credit, manufacturing, and real-estate speculation.[57] Yet even with coffee, in the final instance, control was exercised by US import firms, US government policy, and US coffee consumers.

Colombians thus permanently re-entered the world capitalist economy under the leadership of the most socially regressive, technically advanced elements of their elite. Just as organized labor, in its socialist and anarcho-syndicalist phase, was making itself felt in the rest of the region, Conservative rule was given a new lease of life by the growth of coffee exports. Production jumped from 1 million sacks in 1913 to 2 million in 1921, and 3 million in 1930. After the First World War, foreign capital invested in the coffee sector, and Wall Street opened generous lines of credit in what became known as the "Dance of the Millions" – refreshing the export elite, but bringing no respite to struggling hill-farmers, tenants, and sharecroppers, much less artisans and proletarians. As a result of the report issued by Walter Kemmerer, a Princeton economics professor who led a continent-wide mission to assess the finances of South American governments, US lending dried up in 1927, and capital flight threw the Colombian economy into depression. A decisive shift occurred in elite politics when coffee prices plunged from thirty to seventeen cents a pound in 1929 – a disaster for the export-based economy, consummated in October's Wall Street Crash. The Conservatives split when Church leaders backed rival candidates in succession for the elections of 1930.[58]

III   A New World?

The Antioquian bourgeoisie had "attempted but failed to make Colombia in its own idealized image," and signs of a new popular radicalism were stirring, even as coffee exports reached new heights.[59] The authoritarian politics of the Regeneration and Conservative rule worked by extending property rights to a sector of frontier settlers, and including them in bipartisan networks of patronage and clientelism. This measure of economic democracy reinforced political conservatism, but it left the majority of subalterns – Afro-Colombians, indigenous communities, and many frontier settlers – in the lurch, beyond the reach of the central government, which subordinate groups called on to defend them from landlord power. In 1914, a sharecropper named Quintín Lame was nominated Supreme Leader of the Indigenous Tribes of Colombia, though he did not speak the native language, Nasa. Lame had fought on the Liberal side in the War of a Thousand Days; like other Andean peasant soldiers in this period, he and his movement called for the state to protect non-liberal, collective forms of citizenship in the face of reactionary landlord offensives.[61] Due to his organizing efforts, Lame spent a decade in and out of prison, but the movement he led, known as the *Quintinada*, gained ground through collective land occupations in southern Colombia, passing from Cauca to Tolima in 1922.[62]

The political mood was now markedly different, as anarcho-syndicalist and socialist ideas began to make headway in the labor movement following the Mexican and Russian revolutions and the First World War, and US capital made its first inroads in South America.[63] In 1926, the first political vehicle independent of Liberal and Conservative party tutelage, the Revolutionary Socialist Party (PSR), organized proletarian struggle in the multinational export enclaves of the Caribbean and along coffee frontiers. The PSR's second vice-president, Raúl Eduardo Mahecha – a tailor who, like Quintín Lame, was a Liberal veteran of the War of a Thousand Days – helped found the Oil Workers' Union, USO, and led a strike against Tropical Oil (a Jersey Standard subsidiary) in the Magdalena Medio region in 1926. The party's first vice-president and legendary orator, María Cano, daughter of an oligarchic media family from Medellín, toured the countryside from 1925 to 1927, organizing and agitating for radical change. With Mahecha, Cano led the 4,000-strong banana workers' strike against United Fruit near Santa Marta in November–December 1928.

In the version of the 1928 banana workers' strike immortalized in Gabriel García Márquez's *One Hundred Years of Solitude*, thousands were massacred and loaded onto boxcars, and the memory of the repression erased by official oblivion.[64] In reality, the incident was thoroughly investigated and publicized by a young lawyer recently returned from Mussolini's Italy. A deputy in the Lower House of Congress, Jorge Eliécer Gaitán used the massacre to launch his career as the first populist politician within the Liberal Party, cementing his alliance with left-Liberal *costeños*.[65] In his study of Gaitán, Herbert Braun labeled him, accurately, a petit-bourgeois reformer. But by giving official voice to popular demands and placing the "social question" at the center of national parliamentary debate, Gaitán earned the enmity of the dominant, oligarchic faction of his party, as well as that of the Conservative far right.[66]

In 1929, the PSR's "Bolsheviks of Líbano" rose up in a failed insurrection in northern Tolima; the first explicitly socialist rebellion in Colombia, it represented an alliance formed by radical artisans and provincial intellectuals with tenants, sharecroppers, and smallholders.[66] Indeed, peasants took the offensive, staging land takeovers throughout the coffee axis, and the export proletariat waged its largest strikes to date in the multinational enclaves. Coffee capitalism under Conservative Catholic rule created expectations of property ownership, workers' control, and higher wages that it could not meet, and it crumbled in the face of widespread radical-popular mobilization.

Regions were racialized as relatively privileged sectors of the peasantry were incorporated into networks of patronage and clientelism. Those excluded from the benefits of coffee capitalism mobilized in protest. Indian peasant rebellion spread after 1914, organized labor struck the capitalist enclaves in oil and bananas after 1925, and a wave of multi-ethnic peasant land takeovers swept across the coffee frontiers from 1928. Radical-popular movements achieved greater independence and autonomy from the two parties than in the past, through direct action and the formation of revolutionary Left parties.

3

The Liberal Pause, 1930–46

Colombia was, and continues to be, proof that gradual reform in
the framework of liberal democracy is not the only, or even the
most plausible, alternative to social revolutions, including the ones
that fail or are aborted. I discovered a country in which the failure
to make a social revolution had made violence the constant,
universal, and omnipresent core of public life.

> Eric Hobsbawm, *Interesting Times:*
> *A Twentieth-Century Life* (2002)

Although its effects lasted, the long period of Conservative domination
rested on shaky foundations, and suffered from a basic contradiction: it
gave rise to expectations of property ownership that it could not satisfy.
Ushered in on a wave of mass mobilization, the "Liberal Pause" lasted
from 1930 until 1946. New forces dovetailed with the Left wing of the
Liberal Party – grouped around the charismatic leadership of Jorge
Eliécer Gaitán – to constitute the first radical-popular movement with a
national horizon. Indeed, Gaitán's nationalism was cross-class, multi-
ethnic, and anti-elitist, allowing the Colombian working class to overcome its weakness vis-à-vis capitalist firms and entrepreneurs, on the
basis of its inclusiveness.[67] By 1945, accelerated urbanization, politicized
middle and working classes, and peasant pressure for agrarian reforms led
to a decline in the political weight of landlords throughout the continent.
But in Colombia landlords defeated tenants and sharecroppers, as
industrialists bested organized labor. Whereas elsewhere in the region
mass mobilization created new parties, forced agrarian reform, labor
legislation, or overthrew governments, in Colombia neither urban
populism nor agrarian social democracy lasted as a national force.[68]

I   Incipient Populism

Organized labor, radical peasant movements, the Colombian Communist Party, and Gaitán experimented with organization and mobilization outside the Liberal Party in the first half of the 1930s, before rejoining it in the second half. In conjunction with this new wave of radical-popular mobilization, which now had a national horizon and focus, tepid Liberal agrarian reform and labor legislation met with strong opposition from the Conservative Party. Blessed by the Catholic Church, Conservatives redoubled efforts to rule unopposed in rural areas in order to make up for territory won by Liberals in the cities. This explains why, although social democracy triumphed throughout Latin America at the end of the Second World War, Catholic counterrevolution won the day in Colombia through institutionalized political terror.

With the economic basis of Conservative rule temporarily gone, and their political cohesion broken, the door was left open for Liberals to regain the presidency after fifty years in the wilderness. Their candidate, Olaya Herrera, had been Ambassador in Washington under the Conservatives, with whom he enjoyed good relations, and his vote was less than that of the Conservative rivals combined. There were no startling policy departures. But Gaitán broke from the Liberal Party in 1933 to found the National Union of the Revolutionary Left (UNIR), and approved the founding of peasant leagues to compete with those sponsored by the Liberal Party – and, crucially, with those of the Partido Comunista Colombiano (PCC).[70]

The PCC was founded in 1930 by leaders of the PSR, two of whom, José Gonzalo Sánchez and Dimas Luna, had led the *Quintinada* indigenous movement in the early 1920s. There was continuity with earlier struggles in Cauca and Tolima, and the PCC initially gave priority to peasant struggles on the coffee frontiers, especially in Tolima and Cundinamarca, where the largest plantations were owned by merchant bankers from Bogotá, as well as Germans and North Americans. It set up peasant leagues to capitalize on the wave of land occupations after 1928, and in the early 1930s gained political legitimacy through its "revolutionary agrarianism" based on the "formation and protection of autonomous smallholder communities."[71] Gaitán accused the PCC of skipping stages of historical development: while communist peasant leagues aspired to usher in the socialist revolution, UNIR's were designed to remove the feudal blocks on the development of capitalist agriculture. The countryside was hotly contested political terrain in the early 1930s, and – this was the Comintern's sectarian Third Period – the PCC viewed UNIR as its principal political opponent, especially in Tolima and Cundinamarca.[72]

When Liberals won again – unopposed: the Conservatives boycotted the election – their leader was Alfonso López Pumarejo, the scion of a rich banking family, and a former employee of a US investment firm, Baker-Kellogg. Raised in England and the USA, admirers billed him as the Roosevelt of the Andes. The "Revolution on the March" proclaimed by López was a limited affair, more sweeping in its rhetoric than its reforms, but it raised hopes for populist redistribution and state arbitration of class conflict.[73] Taxation went up, more was spent on schools and roads, and labor legislation was liberalized, which opened the gates to a further growth in unionization, a process that had begun under Olaya. Most importantly, popular expectations of the results of political participation soared.

Effort was invested mainly in revising the Constitution of 1886 to ensure separation of Church and state, but, coupled with the other measures, this was enough to pull Gaitán back into the Liberal fold in 1935. It prompted the PCC, in line with Popular Front policies, to throw its weight behind the López regime, demobilizing its peasant leagues and renouncing its revolutionary vanguardist ambitions.[74] With the support of the PCC, which dominated key trade unions in the transport sector and the export enclaves, López created the Colombian Workers' Confederation (CTC), with the aim of turning organized labor into a clientelist bloc under the control of the Liberal Party.

II Two Steps Back

Though the "Liberal Republic" lasted until 1946, its promise was buried during the second López administration of 1942–45. Embroiled in corruption scandals, López repealed reforms, such as the eight-hour day and social security, which had not been a dead letter for organized labor. He reversed limited land reform in 1944 with Law 100, known as "*la Revancha,*" or "Revenge."[75] Law 100 demonstrated the Liberal Party's inability to resolve "the agrarian question" between peasants and landlords, and highlighted the weight of the latter within the ruling class. The coffee growers' lobby (FENALCO), the landlords' *gremio*, or business lobby (SAC), and the employers' association (APEN) had all pushed for Law 100, which closed the door on sharecropper dreams of independent smallholding. It protected landlord property and labor contracts, pro- hibited the cultivation of crops that would compete in the market, and made it legal to expel sharecroppers and tenants. Older landed groups were able to fashion alliances with the new coffee export elite in order to preserve their privileges. In Cauca, Tolima, and Cundinamarca, where peasant struggle had been vigorous in the 1930s, Law 100 opened the gates for class war from above against mobilized tenants and share- croppers.

An important interpretation has it that the anti-capitalist labor move- ment, allied with peasant and indigenous movements in the 1920s, was co-opted and institutionalized in the 1930s, even as peasant struggle intensified leading up to the passage of Law 200 of 1936. Law 200 was a reform. It established effective occupancy of land as a legal basis for tenure, and it has been argued that this partial victory of coffee workers – it was very partial: landlords benefited far more – in securing access to frontier lands in the 1930s led, ironically, to the isolation of more militant trade unions in other sectors, such as oil and transport. However strong the latter grew, they were unable to affect the central area of the economy. Hence the subsequent fragmentation of the labor movement as a whole, and, in consequence, the strengthening of the two traditional parties. Well before *la Violencia* – so the argument runs – independent class politics had been eclipsed, as smallholders in the coffee belt gained family plots, and were integrated into one of the two parties, while Gaitán and organized labor fit within the Liberal Party fold. During *la Violencia*, intra-class competition to avoid proletarianization, mediated by the clientelist practices and the coffee growers' association, took a fanatically bloody turn, while the urban labor movement was beaten back.

Whereas in other parts of Latin America a mobilized peasantry would play a key role in radical coalitions, after Colombian coffee growers conquered their family plots in the 1930s and 1940s, workers' solidarity disappeared.[75] Although this explains key developments along the coffee axis, it misses the radical challenge *gaitanismo* posed as the first radical- popular movement in Colombian history to unite subordinate groups nationally, across racial, regional, and class divides. It also downplays the importance of *gaitanismo*'s message of class struggle for rural proletarians, tenants, and sharecroppers excluded from property ownership, on the one hand, and the majority of urban workers outside the sphere of organized labor, on the other.[77]

Following the recovery of coffee exports after 1936, and nearly a decade of a 10 per cent annual manufacturing growth, in the early 1940s a consensus emerged among Colombian ruling groups that it was time to return to liberal economic orthodoxy that had prevailed in the capitalist world until the 1930s. Social reforms and pro-labor policies would have no place. In 1944 the city's Conservative manufacturing elite formed ANDI, the national industrialists' organization, and in 1945 coffee merchants founded FEDECAFE. Though they had their differences over the next decade, these groups, joined by intermarriage, subsequently dictated economic policy to successive governments behind the public's back.[78] The Unión de Trabajadores de Colombia (UTC) was set up by the Catholic Church in Medellín in 1946, and was to become the model for organized labor federations.

Liberal Alberto Lleras Camargo, a former Marxist intellectual and Ambassador to Washington, took over when López Pumarejo quit before his time was up, and increased repression of organized labor. In 1945 Lleras Comargo crushed the Communist-led river workers' strike – their union, FEDENAL, had been the most successful in the CTC, and was the only one to achieve a closed shop. Linking the Andean highlands to the Atlantic coast, FEDENAL's workers – sailors, shipwrights, steve-dores, mechanics – carried coffee to the world market; their structural position in the economy gave them the possibility of shutting it down. Their defeat in 1945 represented a major step back for the working class as a whole.

III   Toward *la Violencia*

Gaitán was bound by his own contradictions: he would not leave the Liberal Party, but could not meet the demands of his constituency within the oligarchic bipartisan system. Yet only Gaitán – the leading labor lawyer of the day, who had occupied the posts of senator, city councilor, mayor of Bogotá, minister of education and of labor – contested these developments through official channels, winning a huge following among the Liberal electorate. Though the PCC leadership loathed

him, Gaitán enjoyed support from Communist Party cadres and organized labor – rail, oil, and telecommunications workers backed him
enthusiastically.[79] When the Liberal establishment locked him out of
contention as the party's candidate for the presidency in 1946, he ran on
his own ticket. Though Gaitán took many cities – Bogotá, Barranquilla,
Cali, Cartagena, Cúcuta, Ibagué, Neiva, Santa Marta – the result was to
split the Liberal vote and let the Conservative candidate, Mariano Ospina
Pérez, through, as Conservatives had planned.

The period known simply, though misleadingly, as *la Violencia* – the
defining moment of Colombia's short twentieth century – is often said to
have begun with Gaitán's assassination in 1948. But that is to fore-
shorten it by three years, if not two decades. To understand its roots, it is
necessary to go back to the origins of the Liberal Republic.[80] When
Conservative rule came to an end in 1930, tensions long simmering in
the countryside began to explode. Memories of the partisan slaughter of
the War of a Thousand Days, when Liberal and Conservative notables
mobilized peasant militias to kill each other in a struggle that cost the
lives of one out of every twenty-five Colombians, were still vivid in many
localities. Scarcely had Olaya Herrera taken office when Liberals wreaked
revenge in the Santanders and Boyacá.[81] Conservative fears were thus far
from irrational. Once Liberals were entrenched in power, they resorted
to persistent intimidation, police violence, and fraud. In retaliation,
Conservatives boycotted every presidential election down to 1946. In the
early 1940s, Liberals turned the police into an appendage of their party –
a move that would have dire consequences during *la Violencia*, when the
police were "conservatized." Throughout the "Liberal Pause," there was
a menacing background of killings in the *municipios*, as political
polarization and landlord violence, though still highly localized, spread
incrementally.

If, in Boyacá and the Santanders, the logic of the "defensive feud"
between embattled local communities, each with recollections or fear of
grievous injury, was in place from the beginning, two national developments overdetermined this underlying dynamic.[82] The first was the
shift in the electoral balance between the two parties, once even a
moderate degree of urbanization – and in Colombia it was still quite
moderate – had taken hold. The strength of Conservative loyalties had
depended on the influence of the clergy, which was far stronger in small
towns and the countryside. Once the proportion of city-dwellers passed a

certain threshold in the 1940s, Liberals started to command a permanent majority at the polls. This became clear in the 1946 presidential election itself, which they lost; the two Liberal candidates totaled over 60 per cent of the vote, a level that has been the norm ever since.

On the Conservative side, loss of power had increased the influence of the most extreme wing of the party. Under the charismatic leadership of Laureano Gómez, the party was bent on increasing its rule over the countryside in order to recoup losses in the cities. Dubbed the "creole Hitler" by his foes, Gómez was seen at the time, and has been since, as a fascist demagogue, driving his party to fanatical extremes and plunging the country into civil war. In the ingrown world of the Colombian political elite, he had been a good friend of both López Pumarejo and his successor, Eduardo Santos, and benefited from the former's financial ties. He had solid backing from the key *gremios*, FEDECAFE and ANDI. In the mid-1930s, he had written blistering attacks on both Mussolini and Hitler, but he was a Catholic integrist. Latin America of the 1930s and 1940s was filled with movements and leaders, not all of them reactionary, impressed by the successes of German or Italian fascism: Toro and Busch in Bolivia, Vargas in Brazil, and Perón in Argentina.

What was distinctive in Colombia was that the same kind of attraction pulled Gómez and his party toward Franco, as a traditionalist and religious version of counterrevolution, free of any of the populist connotations of the Italian or German regimes. The result was a rhetorical escalation, to Spanish Civil War levels, of historic enmities toward Liberalism, now represented as indistinguishable from communism. Racist verbal assaults and caricatures of Gaitán – as well as his followers – were unrelenting. Gaitán was known to Bogotá's political elites as "el Negro Gaitán," an epithet that played on his phenotypic features and large Afro-Colombian following in the Caribbean, causes for ridicule and fear. Blacks were "lazy," "unruly," and "immoral." The Hispanophile, Catholic *reconquista* would put them and their leaders – in river, road, and rail workers' unions – in their place.[83]

Like Núñez, seventy years before him, Gómez aimed to return Colombian society to an idealized internal colonial totality in which subalterns knew their proper places, but Gómez lived in the age of total war, and helped push political terror to previously unthinkable levels.

The mid-1940s represented a brief moment of radical-democratic opening almost everywhere in Latin America, with populists swept into power. In Colombia, it saw an aggressive Catholic counterrevolutionary assault on organized labor and radical peasant movements.

4

La Violencia, 1946–57

La violencia is unchained, ordered, and stimulated beyond risk, by remote control. The violence most typical of our political struggles is that which atrociously produces humble victims in the countryside, towns, and city slums . . . But the fuel has been given off by urban desks, worked through with coldness, and astutely elaborated in order to produce its fruits of blood.

Alberto Lleras Camargo (1946)

La Violencia (1946–57) was a mix of "official terror, partisan sectarianism, and scorched earth policy" that resulted from the crisis of the coffee republic, the weakness of the central state, and the contest over property rights. It was distinguished by the "concentrated terror" used to suppress radical-popular politics and confine rising racial/ethnic and class conflict within bipartisan channels.[84] Long a staple of politics in regions and municipalities, violence was first unleashed on the national level against *gaitanista* insurrections, which broke out in the capital and in provincial cities and towns across the country after Gaitán was assassinated in 1948. Appreciation of the threat that the *juntas gaitanistas* posed to central government authority – as well as racial hierarchies and property rights – allows us to register the magnitude of reversal suffered by nascent national-popular forces. *La Violencia* began in the coffee zones of Santander and Boyacá, and was centered in the coffee heartland of northern Valle del Cauca, Viejo Caldas, and Tolima.[85] Mass slaughter took place as it had during the War of a Thousand Days, but the bloodletting lasted longer. Some 300,000 people, 80 per cent men, most of them illiterate peasants, had been killed, and 2 million forcibly displaced, when it officially ended in 1964.[86] It cannot be understood without recognizing the dependent incorporation of the majority of coffee-growers into the clientelist apparatus of each party in smallholding areas of Boyacá, the Santanders, Antioquia, and along the coffee axis.[87]

Colombian participation in the cold war was international, but also domestic: President Laureano Gómez sent Batallón Korea to fight with the US 31st Infantry in 1951, and in 1952, the first group of Colombians trained at the Army Ranger School in Fort Benning, Georgia. Three years later, under General Rojas Pinilla, the US government sponsored chemical warfare – in the form of Colombian-made napalm bombs – against communist "independent republics" in the south. In coordination with US advisors, Colombian veterans of the Korean War led the campaign. It was to be the first of many counter-insurgent failures.

I   The *Bogotazo* as Failed Revolution

Amidst growing sectarian conflict and partisan polarization, in April 1948 President Mariano Ospina Pérez hosted the Ninth Pan-American Congress in Bogotá. Along with Latin American presidents and diplomats, US Secretary of State George C. Marshall attended in order to clarify the role of the USA in the postwar period. Though strengthening regional alliances and establishing the OAS was the ostensible purpose of Secretary Marshall's visit, Washington's chief priority was to maintain its long-standing power and influence in the face of a perceived Soviet "threat." Colombian rulers were eager to be seen as important regional players in world events, and militant anti-communism dovetailed with older creole attitudes toward radical-popular mobilization. This was the combustible setting in which Gaitán was killed.

While attending a conference of anti-imperialist student leaders, Fidel Castro met Gaitán briefly in Bogotá, and the two planned to meet again the following afternoon, 9 April, but Gaitán was assassinated on his way to lunch. News of his murder unleashed the largest urban riots in twentieth-century Colombian history, the so-called *Bogotazo* – a sociopolitical storm that swept the provinces as well as the capital. In the capital, after nearly overwhelming a weakly guarded Presidential Palace, huge crowds from peripheral neighborhoods gathered in the city center. Food rioters against hunger and speculation attacked businesses, especially ones owned by merchants of Middle Eastern origin, and perceived as "foreign." As looting ensued, rioters directly appropriated food, clothing, consumer goods, tools, and hardware. Arsonists torched Church and government buildings, as well as Gómez's newspaper, *El Siglo*. *Gaitanista* professionals and radicalized students from the National University seized radio airwaves, calling for the establishment of revolutionary juntas throughout the country – a reference to the political bodies formed during the wars of independence from Spanish colonialism.

This helped to galvanize the provinces, and after 9 April, radical-popular resistance, organization, and rebellion in areas of recent settlement put the political foundation of the republic in crisis. This was the case in the Magdalena Medio, the valleys of Sinú and San Jorge on the border of Antioquia and Córdoba, as well as northeastern Antioquia, Cali, northern Valle, Cundinamarca, and Tolima. Organized labor established revolutionary juntas in Bogotá, Cali, Remedios, Zaragoza, Puerto Berrío, Barrancabermeja, and dozens of *municipios*.[88] Even though goals were modest, popular mobilization after Gaitán's death was so intense and widespread as to "transform" the "reformist content" of the demands. In terms of power and authority, the world was briefly turned upside down: the persecuted became the powerful, prisoners executed guards, police took the side of the *pueblo gaitanista*, peasants rustled cattle and took over land, and oil workers held the refinery in Barranca. Insurgents spoke of a revolutionary new order backed by popular militias.[89]

Lacking support from the capital, and isolated from one another, the juntas were quickly vanquished, however. Although the *Bogotazo* was an expression of popular rage, it did not lead to a seizure of power, except in the provinces, and then briefly. The populism Gaitán sketched on the left flank of Liberalism was a growing threat to the country's oligarchy, which he named as such. Viewed comparatively, though, it was still relatively weak. The dispersal of the big-city population into at least four regional centers, Bogotá, Medellín, Cali, and Barranquilla, none of which had over half a million inhabitants by 1940, deprived a potential Colombian populism of a critical mass of urban, working-class organization. Gaitán himself noted, in 1943, that less than 5 per cent of the country's workforce was unionized, and though juntas took power around the country, they could not hold it. Secretary Marshall saw the Soviet Union and its tool, "international communism," as the invisible hand directing the *Bogotazo*. Fidel Castro left for Cuba on

10 April, but offered a different interpretation: "No one can claim to have organized what happened on April 9 because what was absent on April 9 was precisely that, organization. This is the key: there was absolutely no organization."[90] Without preparation, leadership, or a program for self-government, *gaitanista* insurrections could not have led to revolution.[91] Yet in light of new studies, the classic view of *La Violencia* as a reaction against the radical thrust of *gaitanismo* is persuasive.[92]

II   *La Resistencia* and *La Reconquista*

Instead, partisan conflict spread across the coffee axis, following the precedent set in Boyacá and the Santanders, beginning in 1945. Liberal notables in coffee districts of Quindío and Tolima, fearing Conservative revenge for the upheaval – which materialized in a wave of local assassinations – mobilized peasant clients into guerrilla militias, hoping for an outcome different from the War of a Thousand Days. Unlike nineteenth-century military conflicts, dominated by oligarchic leaders, during *la Violencia* Liberal commanders were peasants, with *noms de guerre* like "Sangrenegra" (Blackblood) and "Capitán Desquite" (Captain Vengeance).

The goal of these Liberal-communist guerrillas was to overthrow Conservative government, not establish a new society. Yet this resistance further ignited the counterrevolution in the countryside. "Order" was restored in the capital when troops and volunteers came from nearby Conservative Boyacá to reinforce the Army, which remained loyal to Conservatives. The volunteers, known as *chulavitas*, were at first used locally in Chulavita County in Boyacá, where Liberal violence had been widespread in the 1930s: but in 1949, Liberal presidential candidate, Darío Echandía, was assassinated in Bogotá. Thus Conservatives used *chulavitas* in Boyacá and the capital during and after the *Bogotazo*, and, later, in the coffee axis further south: Tolima, Valle del Cauca, and Viejo Caldas (Caldas, Risaralda, Quindío). *Chulavitas* were devoted to the Virgin of Carmen, as theirs was a "holy war" to rid the countryside of atheists, masons, and communists – in a word, Liberals.[93]

Backed by the clergy, in Antioquia, Gómez's Catholic legions mobilized to "conservatize" municipalities before upcoming elections; in Nariño they did the same. Those from Nariño, in turn, were recruited to help conservatize northern Valle, where Conservative advance was total. Liberal communities defected en masse in self-preservation once Conservative "civil police" replaced Liberal police in 1947–48, and were then organized into a professional force of political assassins in 1949–50.

When war broke out after Gaitán's death, the PSD – already outlawed by Ospina – focused on clandestine work in the countryside, advocating armed self-defense.[94] In 1949 its first groups formed along the railway line in Santander, in the oil enclaves of Shell, Socony, and Tropical Oil in Northern Santander and Ariari; and, most importantly, given the subsequent course of events, in Tolima and Cundinamarca, where the PCC and UNIR's peasant leagues had been strongest in the 1930s. At the end of the year, Liberal chieftains, backed by the departmental governor, as well as leading merchant-landlords, approached the party for help in setting up guerrillas. By 1950, with official sectarianism operating at a feverish pitch, *gaitanistas* formed a guerrilla front with PSD fighters in southern Tolima. The force was led by the Loayza clan, one of whose members, Pedro Antonio Marín, a.k.a. Manuel Marulanda, or "Tirofijo" (Sure Shot), leads the FARC today.[95]

The response to 9 April and the revolutionary juntas was barbarous reprisal: Conservatives cut out the tongues and eyes of at least forty Liberals, and disemboweled others in San Rafael in Valle del Cauca, for example. *Gaitanista* county seats – there had been many in Valle in 1948 – were subject to "little jobs" (*trabajitos*), or selective assassinations, carried out by *los pájaros*. These were birdlike killers working for Conservatives, who circulated in black cars without plates, and "flew back" to daily life in the towns as devout Catholic butchers, drivers, bartenders, tailors, laundrymen, or police inspectors. Their leader, León María Lozano, "El Cóndor," began his participation in *la Violencia* with the defense of a chapel – where he had erected a shrine to the Virgen María Auxiliadora – against *gaitanistas* in Cali. He would soon run the largest, most well-protected gang of Conservative Catholic gunmen in northern Valle. He brought in professionals from Boyacá, Antioquia, Santander, Tolima, or Quindío, but recruited others from hamlets and *municipios* around Tuluá.

When he was a colonel in charge of the Third Brigade in Valle, Gustavo Rojas Pinilla appeared with El Cóndor in a photograph. Rojas Pinilla and the Conservative governor planned the suppression of the *gaitanista* revolt that had taken over Cali's Palacio de San Francisco. This was an important step in Rojas's political ascent, which he secured by putting down *juntas revolucionarias* throughout the department. Thereafter, Lozano and the *pájaros*, working with secret police, terrorized the region. Under *laureanista* Governor Nicolás Borrero Olano, owner of the right-wing daily, *Diario del Pacífico*, Rojas Pinilla's declaration of "neutrality" in the face of spreading *pájaro* violence allowed free circulation of anonymous killers hired to murder Liberals. Military "neutrality" was essential to the success of the "little jobs," or assassinations, in which the new Conservative police participated in gangs of three or four, with *pájaros*. Coffee and cattle merchants, as well as medium-sized landowners, rose in their shadow.[96]

El Cóndor was only the most legendary of those in the business of political assassinations; he had counterparts in Viejo Caldas and Tolima. As in Viejo Caldas, the business of *la Violencia* in northern Valle and Tolima created avenues for upward mobility for middle sectors. The networks of patronage and protection in which the *pájaros* moved were run by politicians who filled important legislative, diplomatic, and ministerial posts after *la Violencia* ended.[97]

The more "the partisan content of oppositions was emphasized, the more these were stripped of their political potential," which led to the "disaggregation, disorganization, and disarticulation" of radical-popular forces.[98] In vain, the Liberal oligarchy, at the suggestion of López Pumarejo and the insistence of Carlos Lleras Restrepo, tried to recuperate the broken bipartisan consensus. In Bogotá, the Liberal newspaper, *El Tiempo*, as well as the houses of Lleras Restrepo and López Pumarejo, were torched by Conservatives in 1949, demonstrating the impossibility of slowing the momentum of Conservative extremism.[99] In coffee smallholding zones, the aim was not to achieve victory on the battlefield, but to expel the enemy from the region. Conquest of territory – the accumulation of land, livestock, and coffee – was the goal, and killing obeyed a sinister calculus of pain and cruelty. Pregnant women were disemboweled and fetuses destroyed, so new members of the opposite party would not be born.

In Tolima, different cuts were used to send messages. In the "necktie cut," the victim's tongue was pulled down through an opening in the throat; in the "florists' cut," severed limbs were inserted in the neck after decapitation; in the "monkey's cut," the victim's head was placed on his or her chest.[100] Mutilation of ears, fingers, penises, and breasts were common, as were rapes. Tens of thousands were disemboweled and thrown into rivers like the Cauca, which was said to have run red with blood. Arson was another common tool of terror, and millions of peasants either watched their houses and crops burn or left them behind.

In Antioquia, where bipartisan consensus was a well-established elite tradition, levels of violence were lower than in the coffee regions of Valle del Cauca, Viejo Caldas, and Tolima. Political radicalism, internal colonialism, and the location of natural resources largely determined when and where state-sanctioned terror escalated without limits. During the second phase (1950–53) of *la Violencia*, those who lived on regional peripheries differed from accepted cultural norms of whiteness in the Antioquian heartland. They suffered the consequences of army and police violence – or, in the east and Urabá, privatized landlord violence – to a degree unknown during the first phase (1945–49), which had been centered in southern and southwestern coffee municipalities like Fredonia. There, conflict was kept within strict, bipartisan limits, designed to "conservatize" Liberal municipalities located in Conservative areas. Middle-class politicians, journalists, and intellectuals helped polarize politics along bipartisan lines.

In the second phase, Laureano Gómez, elected president in 1950, was determined to prevent a repetition of the *Bogotazo* and its provincial variants. Once *laureanistas* took over, violence in Antioquia was concentrated in geographically peripheral, but economically strategic regions, where Afro-Colombian majorities – organized in the 1940s as *gaitanista* railroad workers, miners, and road workers – supported radical opposition politics and armed insurgency. There, the central and regional state's institutional presence was limited to the police and armed forces. Where these proved ineffective, as in Urabá and the east (the Lower Cauca, Magdalena Medio, and the northeast), power was transferred to the *contrachusma* – parastate forces that, set in motion, proved even more difficult for Conservative elites to manage than police and the armed forces.

Gómez withdrew due to poor health soon after his term began, and Roberto Urdaneta Arbeláez became the titular head of government in October 1951, as *la Violencia* took on a greater intensity, appeared in new forms, and affected new regions. Gómez was the first president whose national program sanctioned the most reactionary developments in the regions. The peasantry suffered the brunt of state violence: recently returned from Korea, for example, Batallón Colombia massacred 1,500 peasants in a rural area outside El Líbano, Tolima, in 1952.

Clientelist co-optation of smallholding petty producers through civil war in the coffee axis could not put a stop to independent class politics altogether, but it did shift their geography toward more recently settled frontiers. The eastern plains, for example, evolved toward an embryonic agrarian revolutionary society in 1952–53. Law 1 was issued in September 1952, after a meeting of delegates from the country's guerrilla organizations in "Red Viotá" (Cundinamarca) in August, which then became the First National Conference of the Popular Movement of National Liberation. It organized a rudimentary justice system under self-designated civilian and military authorities, stipulating rules for land use, as well as individual rights and obligations regarding community labor. It set up guidelines for the establishment of dairy farms and "revolutionary" agrarian settlements, and regulated the cattle market – the economic lifeblood of the eastern plains. As efforts to establish a national guerrilla coordination advanced, Law 2 of the Eastern Plains, written by José Alvear Restrepo, regulated life in the vast liberated zones, and sketched designs for revolution and a popular government.[100]

The law established a government of popular assemblies and district councils in charge of planning production, consumption, and distribution. It laid down rules regarding the relations between combatants and civilians, expressly prohibiting torture and the scorched-earth policies that marked *la Violencia*, and mandating civilized behavior toward Conservatives. Communist enclaves were the only territories where life was *not* regulated by terror. Law 2 also addressed civil marriage, divorce, women's equality, and indigenous rights. Laws 1 and 2 of the Eastern Plains represented "the most complete democratic project proposed by the armed movement."[102]

III   Cold War Dictatorship

When Gómez attempted to resume his duties in 1953, he was ousted by Colombia's only military coup of modern times, in part because the Conservatives had split between extremists and moderates. The latter abhorred the parastate *contrachusma* and its variants, as well as the generalized persecution and criminalization of upstanding Liberal citizens. General Rojas Pinilla, now head of the Army, seized power with the support of Gómez's factional opponents within the Conservative Party, with which he had close family and personal connections. He set about molding organized labor into a clientelist bloc. His anti-oligarchic, nationalist discourse has led some scholars to see him as a figure similar to Argentina's Juan Perón. But Rojas Pinilla participated in the Conservative bloodletting as a commander – even the US Embassy complained that he "saw a red behind every coffee bush" – and, as president, amassed a fortune in crooked cattle and real-estate deals.[103] He also personally intervened to free El Cóndor, leader of the *pájaros*, from jail in Buga.

With heavier and more decentralized repression, rural violence was far from extinguished under Rojas Pinilla. Beginning with Gómez, violence had become part of central government policy. No longer exclusively regional, it had become a national terror that increased rather than decreased after the "guerrilla threat" was absent. The foundations of the cold war national security state were erected earlier in Colombia than anywhere else in Latin America, since they meshed with creole traditions of partisan sectarianism.

Under Gómez, partisan sectarianism had begun to open the fault lines of the bipartisan system itself, however; and, to the delight of Liberals, Rojas Pinilla made "reconciliation" between the two parties his first priority. Toward that end, his most significant act as president was to declare a general amnesty for Liberal guerrillas. The first demobilization, backed by merchants, landlords, and political bosses, took place in central Tolima. It was widely publicized as a means of enticing guerrilla chiefs in northern and southern Tolima to follow, which they did. Commanders like Rafael Rangel, who operated in the Magdalena Medio, and Captain Franco Yepes in Antioquia, were not far behind. After five years of fighting, the strongest Liberal guerrillas, a force of some 10,000 on the eastern plains, turned over their arms, under the leadership of Guadelupe Salcedo.

The movement of armed Left resistance fragmented in response to Rojas Pinilla's offer, and after guerrillas from the eastern plains demobilized, wind was taken from revolutionary sails. Under intensified military pressure, some communist militias demobilized. In southern Tolima, a zone characterized by decentralized leadership, a micro-war unfolded between former allies, as Liberals – now reintegrated into the party apparatus – succeeded in expelling the communists from much of the region.

Those who had displayed an "exaggerated support or adhesion" to the Gómez regime were amnestied in June 1954. To stamp out one of the remaining communist redoubts, though, Rojas Pinilla unleashed the War of Villarica in 1955. Batallón Colombia, the veterans of Korea, targeted a highland municipality of northern Tolima that had been home to peasant unions and the Communists' Democratic Front for National Liberation. Rojas Pinilla ordered a blitz of 5,000 troops, with US-donated F-47s and B-26 bombers, and a torture center, known as "the Cunday Concentration Camp," was established. Napalm was sprayed on the "target area," as in Korea, and it was occupied by government forces. An estimated 100,000 peasants were displaced. Half the communist guerrillas fled to Sumapaz, across the border in Cundinamarca. Another column, with 100 armed men and 200 families, made the legendary "long march" over the eastern cordillera into the lowlands, to found the settlements of El Guayabero in western Meta and El Pato in north-western Caquetá, as trade union or peasant leaders in the mountains became military commanders in new colonies on the frontier.[104]

Overall, *la Violencia* was a huge historical regression, in which partisan hostilities swamped not only the legacy of Gaitán's populism, but also the chance of mass-based independent class politics beyond it.[105] It spawned new modes of terror. In the nineteenth century, terms of military engagement were agreed upon, but during *la Violencia*, neither rules nor limits obtained – elderly men, women, and children were frequently targeted.[106] Although its geography largely coincided with the coffee frontiers settled in the late nineteenth and early twentieth centuries – as the case of Antioquia demonstrates – *la Violencia* was about more than a generalized escalation of bipartisan competition and conflict over patronage, votes, land, labor power, and commodities.[107] In Antioquia, internal colonialism and the racialization of regional peripheries through terror and expropriation were crucial in beating back the tide of *gaitanismo*.

Though *la Violencia* received a decisive push nationally with the election of Laureano Gómez as president in 1950, it was orchestrated and controlled at the subnational levels. Regional guerrilla movements, some of which left offshoots that grew into durable communist insurgencies during the cold war, formed in alliance with the Liberal Party throughout the country. Conservative parastate forces took over many county seats and village hamlets. Through "the agrarian question," the Liberal Party had made important inroads in rural districts in the 1930s and 1940s, challenging Conservative dominance of the countryside for the first time since the 1870s.[107] Like the Regeneration seventy years before it, Gómez's *reconquista* aimed to return Colombian society to an idealized internal colonial totality in which subalterns knew their places.

It was during *la Violencia* that the precedent for the bloody resolution of the agrarian question, through terror, expropriation, and dispossession, was established. Forms of cruelty that became widespread in late twentieth-century Colombia were institutionalized in Latin America's most regressive historical development at mid-century. They persisted as part of the cold war counterinsurgent repertoire, helping prepare the ground for endemic Left insurgency.

5

The National Front:
Political Lockout, 1957–82

Is there no way that Colombia, instead of killing its sons, can make them dignified to live? If Colombia cannot respond to this question, I prophecy a curse: "Desquite" will come back to life, and the earth will be spilled with blood, pain, and tears.

Gonzalo Arango (1966)

National Front agreements signed in 1958 rebuilt the coffee republic on an axis that revolved around the Liberal Party, with vanquished Conservatives given half the spoils, and radical-popular expressions banned. Forgetting was the "central leitmotif" of the period, and the effect was to "kill the memory" of *la Violencia*.[109] The historical profession contributed to this state of affairs with its "private commitment to create collective amnesia."[110] Growth without equity reigned, patterns of inequality were maintained or deepened, and clientelism was recreated.[111] When US-sponsored, right-wing military dictatorships swept Latin America during the 1960s and 1970s, Colombia was held up as a showpiece of democracy in the struggle for the "free world." In contrast to Venezuela, whose political system was also praised during the cold war, the Colombian state succeeded neither in neutralizing nor defeating its guerrilla insurgencies, intact since the 1960s. In part, their longevity is due to the exclusion of popular – particularly peasant – demands from the mainstream political system.

I   Counterinsurgency

When Rojas Pinilla made clear his intention of staying in power indefinitely, cracking down on opponents and simulating populist gestures for urban consumption, the oligarchy, which had always prized civilian rule, closed ranks. They were especially threatened by his attempt to control patronage and build independent clientelist bases. By early 1957, not only both political parties, but industrialists, coffee exporters, and the Church wanted him out; a business-organized shutdown toppled him. Two months later, Gómez – exiled in Franco's Spain – signed the Pact of Sitges with Alberto Lleras Camargo.

This formally committed Conservatives and Liberals to create a National Front that would share power equally between the two parties, with alternating occupation of the presidency and parity of representation at all levels of government. Supported by business leaders, the Church and party elites, the pact was scheduled to last until 1974; in practice, it endured, with minor modifications, until 1990. The Church, abandoning its exclusive affiliation with the Conservative Party, sought to unify the two formations.[112]

Hopes for unity among the nation's armed peasant groups across the eastern cordillera died when Guadelupe Salcedo was assassinated in Bogotá in 1957, and though Laureano Gómez did not last as president, he returned, politically triumphant, in 1958 to preside over the Senate, where he put Rojas Pinilla on trial. Since anti-communism was a pillar of the world view he expressed as a political columnist, Conservative Party leader, and president, his paranoid obsessions with "masons" and "atheists" were now tolerated. Like Rojas Pinilla, Gómez helped to institutionalize impunity for government-sanctioned political violence. He was thus the true victor in the contests of *la Violencia*. The 1950s were like a nightmarish return to the nineteenth century, but Gómez and his followers were very much of the twentieth.[113] Theirs was a merciless, enforced forgetting, based on historical myth and fantasies of total dominance.

The traditional two-party system had stunted and twisted the expression of political oppositions, but could not repress them altogether. In the 1930s and 1940s, in a replay of the nineteenth-century period of Liberal hegemony (1862–75), an incipient left-populist dynamic developed, and Conservatism was reinforced by a flamboyant defense of private property, the family, and the altar. In their way, each of these had escaped elite control, unleashing a sectarian conflict worse than the War of a Thousand Days, which eventually came to threaten the diarchy itself. The National Front restored the two-party system, now drained of any real tension between its components. In cold war conditions in Colombia, the New Deal had been buried, and the Cruzada Nacionalista was melded with a shared referent, anti-communism, that was sufficient unifying cement for the two parties.

The result was to proscribe political expression of radical and reformist demands, as the state became a machinery of common elite interests that apportioned all government offices and posts to Liberals and Conservatives in advance. Coffee exports provided the basis of state budgets and subsidized a protected domestic industry. As early as 1941, the private organization of the coffee growers, FEDECAFE, began to direct the National Coffee Fund without public oversight, and this arrangement continued through the 1970s. In spite of the interventionist regulatory mechanisms introduced by López Pumarejo in the 1930s and 1940s, the Liberal state became an executive committee of the bourgeoisie, but one that had no hegemonic fraction and no national project.[114]

Regional and local political power remained more important than central government authority in most places, and though it had been officially forgotten, "the Violence . . . formed the substance of rural and small-town life" through the early National Front.[115] The effects were particularly evidenced by the proliferation of banditry: Conservatives, like Efraín González, led gangs of young men who roamed the central and western cordilleras attempting to avenge the deaths of loved ones through atrocity. Just as Liberal guerrillas and Conservative *contrachusma* had never confronted one another during the second phase of *la Violencia* in Antioquia (1950–53), the same was true of González and Capitán Desquite, the bandit captain hired by Liberal coffee hacienda owners in Quindío to stop Efraín González – the one whom Antioquian writer Gonzalo Arango mentions in the epigraph. The *bandoleros* and *cuadrillas* moved back and forth, from the western to the central cordillera, between Quindío and Tolima. With several exceptions, bandits in the coffee axis did not last under National Front arrangements. The Colombian Armed Forces, led by the army's Batallón Colombia, which was supported by US military advisors, training, and funding, eliminated them.[116]

Radical-popular movements under the National Front were criminalized by state-of-siege legislation that equated protest with subversion. Quasi-official opposition forces, such as the Revolutionary Liberal Movement (MRL), led by Alfonso López Michelsen, had support in the countryside, and the Alianza Nacional Popular (ANAPO), led by Rojas Pinilla after his return from exile, had a growing base in the cities. Both had to run candidates on Liberal or Conservative slates. The MRL brought together Marxist intellectuals, radical writers, students, excluded public sector workers, and modernizing bureaucrats with peasants. ANAPO, in which the Conservative bandit Efraín González participated actively until his death in 1965, was classic right-wing populism: anti-imperialism combined with attacks on birth control and, later, support for Pablo VI's Papal Encyclical of 1968. Banned from elections, communists fell into line behind the Liberal Party, which constituted the "spinal column" of National Front politics, as the pattern established under López was institutionalized.[117]

Low electoral participation rates were an invariant feature of the National Front. If Colombia was spared the experience of the military dictatorships that decimated middle-class, labor, and peasant radicalism elsewhere in Latin America during the 1960s and 1970s, it is because the National Front was a semi-authoritarian parliamentary dictatorship. Though labor militancy increased in the mid-1960s, in a rapidly deteriorating economic situation caused by falling coffee prices, the labor movement remained fragmented and weak after *la Violencia*. With the closure of political space in the civilian arena blocking the re-emergence of vibrant urban populism centered on the trade unions, one avenue for social protest seemed available.

In the 1960s and 1970s, just as the country's majority went from being rural to urban, the vehicle of choice for opposition forces became rural insurgency. This was rooted in the long prehistory of the peasant struggles and land occupations along the coffee frontier, and their engulfing by the larger turbulence of *la Violencia*, which lingered as banditry through the early years of the National Front. But there were also still enclaves of communist resistance. In 1961, Laureano Gómez's son, Álvaro, at that time a senator, coined the term "independent republics" to refer to sixteen areas over which the central government did not exercise territorial sovereignty. Under the Liberal presidency of Lleras Camargo – who crushed the 1945 river-workers' strike and was handpicked by Laureano Gómez as the National Front candidate in 1958 – these "red zones" were surrounded by a military cordon that effectively isolated them from the outside world.

Once the Cuban Revolution put Washington into high gear, there was a new urgency to eradicate guerrilla forces in Colombia. During the Alliance for Progress, anti-communist counterinsurgency moved into its second phase, as the mission of Latin American militaries changed from "hemispheric defense" to "national security."[118] The "external threat" from the Soviet Union was to be handled by the USA, as demonstrated in the Cuban missile crisis; while the "internal threat" of communist subversion would be managed by the police and armed forces of a given country. An early veteran of Vietnam, Colonel William Yarborough, headed the Special Warfare Center at Fort Bragg, and led a military mission to Colombia in 1962, and complained of its lack of preparation and professionalism, recommending the organization of local death squads accountable only to the US government.[119]

A territorially fragmented counterinsurgency confronted agrarian reform when President Lleras Camargo founded a government bureaucracy, Incora, in 1961, to be run by the president's cousin, Senator Carlos Lleras Restrepo, who formed a corps of young economists, many of them US-educated. Their power within the state was still nascent, and confined to Incora. But their vision of progress entailed the elimination of the large estate, seen as backward and unproductive, and the conversion of "serfs" into a yeoman citizenry.[120] The reform process continued under Guillermo Valencia, a poet from the former colonial slaveholding city, Popayán, but Valencia sympathized with General Franco and the Spanish Falange, and one of his principal campaign promises was to eliminate "independent republics." After steady industrial and commercial growth through the 1950s, in 1962, economic crisis, due to falling coffee prices, led to the lowest rates of industrial growth since the early 1930s, and after 1964 urban unemployment became widespread. Future fractures in the National Front were thereby guaranteed.

Plan Lazo, a "hearts-and-minds" counterinsurgent strategy that had at its core a military-civilian force and specialized units, designed to hunt and kill alleged communist supporters, determined that civilians would be either collaborators or targets.[121] As General Alberto Ruíz Novoa explained at the Conference of American Armed Forces in the Panama Canal Zone in 1963, the only way to defeat the insurgencies was by mobilizing and militarizing rural communities through "civic-military action."[122] Ruíz Novoa had been the commander of Batallón Colombia in Korea, and fought the Chinese People's Liberation Army with the Polar Bears of the US Army's 31st Infantry.

Ruíz was convinced that, in order to defeat Colombian peasant guerrillas, it would be necessary to drain the sea in which they swam. To do so, the state would have to invest in regions of communist influence, as well as enlist civilian collaboration with the armed forces. General Ruíz thought of these "peasant self-defense" forces as an elite group, trained to coordinate with the army, particularly in intelligence work – similar to what Colonel Yarborough recommended, but answerable to Colombian authority. Ruíz's plan, known as Plan Lazo, would isolate the guerrillas from their potential support base by improving infrastructure, health, and education.[123]

II Insurgency

National Front counterinsurgency operations unleashed a wave of armed migrations, from the central highlands to the southern jungles and eastern plains. In late May 1964, Plan Lazo failed dramatically when, in coordination with its US allies, the Colombian Armed Forces launched "Operación Marquetalia" (Operation Sovereignty), to retake the municipality of Marquetalia, a communist hamlet in the extreme south of Tolima, on the border of Cauca and Huila. Another Korean veteran, Lieutenant Colonel José Joaquín Matallana, led an assault that featured the use of Huey helicopters, T-33 combat planes, seven army battalions, two specialized counterinsurgent companies, and intelligence groups (GIL), designed to wipe out the community and its now legendary leader, Tirofijo. Here, and in other coordinated military attacks, territory was captured, but only briefly; "the enemy" remained at large. After Marquetalia, families forced to flee once more found their way either to the Cauca or into the tropical lowlands of Caquetá and Meta. Unable to settle in their villages, fighters formed a guerrilla column.

Both Matallana and Tirofijo agreed that Marquetalia forced agrarian communists to cease being a sedentary self-defense militia and become a mobile force.[124] US advisors had supervised "Operation Sovereignty" at a nearby military base, but soon after it was launched, comandantes from Marquetalia, Río Chiquito, and El Pato came together, as the Bloque Sur, to issue a new agrarian program. This "people's response to violence and militarist aggression" was later to be commemorated as the birth of the FARC, officially named in 1966. According to their historian, through the 1970s, the FARC functioned as a "regional structure of social warfare, of individual and collective survival," and developed in "a setting for the building of real local power."[125] The secret of the FARC's early success was the subordination of insurgent organizational goals to demands and movements of frontier smallholders, tenants, and rural laborers.

This emerges especially clearly in comparison with competitors on the Left, for two other guerrilla forces emerged in these years. The ELN is usually characterized as a middle-class, university-based group that followed Che's theory of the *foco* to the letter. It was convinced that, given the size of Colombia's peasantry, and its recent history of armed popular mobilization during *la Violencia*, a small band of mobile guerrillas – in place of the working class and the peasantry – could trigger an insurrection that would lead to socialist revolution. This was typical of groups that followed Guevara in these years: for them, revolution was an act of consciousness and will, capable of overcoming material and political determinations.

Strategic differences aside, however, the ELN was no less rooted in the history of popular liberalism, communism, and peasant-proletarian struggle than the FARC. The patriarch of the Vásquez clan had participated in the *gaitanista* takeover of the country's oil port, Barrancabermeja, in 1948, and led Liberal militias under Rafael Rangel during *la Violencia*, where he met his death. The Vásquez brothers, Fabio and Manuel, went to Cuba with a small group of scholarship students during the Cuban missile crisis in 1962. On their return, they set up the first ELN *foco* in San Vicente de Chucurí, Santander, where Rangel's guerrillas had been active, as Liberal guerrillas in the War of a Thousand Days had been before them.

The ELN counted on support from sectors from the Oil Workers' Union, USO, following the strike against the newly formed state petroleum company, ECOPETROL, in 1963, as well as elderly peasant squatters who had led the "Bolshevik Uprising" in El Líbano, Tolima, in 1929, and *juntas gaitanistas* in 1948. Some early cadres had fought under Rangel, while Fabio Vásquez started out in the youth wing of the MRL, looking for a way to avenge his father's death. Others, like Manuel Vásquez and Rodrigo Lara, came to the guerrillas via student struggle at the Universidad Industrial in Bucaramanga. The ELN announced its presence with the "takeover of Simacota," a town in Santander, in January 1965, and later that year accepted priest and sociologist Camilo

Torres Restrepo, who was promptly sent to his death in combat in early 1966. This provided liberation theology with its first martyr.[126]

In 1967, the Maoist People's Liberation Army (EPL) was formed out of this matrix of armed agrarian radicalism. One of its founders, Pedro Vázquez Rendón, had been the PSD's political commissar in southern Tolima during *la Violencia* – he suggested that Pedro Antonio Marín call himself Manuel Marulanda, in honor of one of the leaders of the PSR in the 1920s. The PCC-ML (Communist Party-Marxist-Leninist) emerged from the youth wing of the PCC in 1965, following the Sino-Soviet split. With the help of former Liberal guerrilla commander and MRL militant, Julio Guerra, the EPL set up a *foco* in Urabá with the goal of waging prolonged popular war. As Maoists, they believed that in rural "Third World" countries like Colombia, the peasantry, led by a vanguard party, would play the leading role in making socialist revolution.[127]

In spite of the internationalist patina imported from Moscow and Beijing, the unfinished business of *la Violencia* gave rise to all three Left insurgencies. Like much of the rest of small-town and rural Colombian society, *la guerrilla* continued to be marked by the experience of *la Violencia*, decades after it officially ended. Quindío and Risaralda, for example, were coffee regions that had been home to Conservative gunmen and Liberal bandit gangs, as well as the Vásquez family and Tirofijo. Kidnapping, *la vacuna* ("the vaccination," a form of protection rent), and *el boleteo* (the charging of war taxes via threatening letters), first developed in Viejo Caldas and northern Valle. Given new names (*la retención, el impuesto de guerra*), they were incorporated into the repertoire of guerrilla tactics.

Both Fabio Vásquez and Tirofijo saw their fathers murdered by Conservatives, and personal vendettas gave the guerrilla movements continuity with *la Violencia*. So did Ricardo Franco and Eribito Espitia, who had both been with the regional Liberal bandit chieftain, "Chispas," before going their separate ways. Espitia was a founding member of the ELN, and Franco became the commander of the FARC's IV Front in the Middle Magdalena.[128]

In order to ward off what was correctly perceived to be a threat of rising conflict in the countryside, President Carlos Lleras Restrepo (1966–70) – who had been one of Gaitán's staunchest opponents in the Liberal Party, and presided over his funeral – instituted a new agrarian reform program. Lleras also created a peasant organization, the

National Association of Peasant Users (ANUC), to drum up clientelist support for the initiative.[129] It moved in radical directions, far beyond what Lleras Restrepo and the Liberal technocrats had envisioned, especially along the Atlantic coast, where *latifundismo* was most extensive.[130] Under Valencia's Decree 3398, in 1965, and Law 48, passed by Congress in 1968, however, regionally based landlords organized death squads on the model of *los pájaros*, and targeted the student and labor Left for selective assassination in the cities.[131] This continuity was matched by a similar continuity in the counterinsurgency, whose vision of total war on civilians was refined and systematized in the cold war.

III Counter-reform, Repression, Resurrection

The ideological audacity and relative popular legitimacy of the guerrilla groups should not lead us to exaggerate their size, nor to overlook the rapid demographic shift from country to city in these years. By the mid-1970s, the EPL was practically non-existent; Fabio Vásquez spent the early years purging the ELN's meager ranks, and the *foquistas* were nearly eliminated by an onslaught of 30,000 troops at Anorí, Antioquia in 1973. The FARC were still confined mainly to the lowland regions southeast of Bogotá, which they had helped to colonize. In the cities, meanwhile, where two-thirds of Colombians now lived, though secondary education and health care expanded, unemployment rose sharply during the 1960s. Protectionist industrial policies failed to generate jobs, so the working and lower-middle class saw hopes of social mobility dashed. In 1969 ANAPO won majorities in municipal councils and departmental assemblies.

Deterioration of the edifice of the National Front was clearly visible. In 1970 Rojas Pinilla, running as a Conservative on an anti-National Front platform, mobilized an anti-oligarchic discourse reminiscent of Gaitán's – supplemented by a reactionary defense of a Catholic tradition that was gradually losing ground to mass-media influence – to win an estimated 39 per cent of the vote, mainly from the lower-middle and working class. The National Front resorted to thinly disguised last-minute fraud to deny him victory and impose its own candidate, Conservative Misael Pastrana.

Once in office, Pastrana sponsored public works and urban remodeling in an attempt to generate employment and the appearance of reform, but he also supported a process of counter-reform in the countryside. Cattle ranchers (FEDEGAN), agribusiness and landlords (SAC), as well as industrialists (ANDI), were united in their determination to roll back reforms initiated under Lleras Restrepo – or, as in Urabá, to turn them to their advantage, just as landlords had done with Law 200 in 1936. The reaction was a response to ANUC land takeovers that swept Boyacá, Tolima, Huila, Valle del Cauca, the Magdalena Medio, the eastern plains, and the Atlantic coast. In 1971, in Toribío, Cauca, the Regional Indigenous Council of Cauca was formed to craft local development proposals based on recuperation of community reserves (*resguardos*) that had been incorporated into large, privately held estates. While defining their goal as the attainment of indigenous autonomy, members of CRIC self-consciously built on the struggles of Quintín Lame and the PCC. They therefore focused on land as the basis of collective life and culture, local self-government through *cabildos*, and the formation of broad, national-popular alliances with intellectuals, workers, and especially non-indigenous peasants, in order to overcome regional, ethnic, and class barriers to unity.[132] On the border of Urabá, in areas of extensive cattle ranching in the Sinú Valley in Córdoba, where *gaitanista* resistance had been strong in 1948, and in neighboring Sucre, ANUC led a third of all marches and land takeovers undertaken nationwide between 1970 and 1973. The area along the Atlantic coast was thus the hotbed of agrarian struggle in this period. Frustrated with the limits of reform under Lleras, ANUC had the firm backing of Left parties, a vigorous university movement protesting the privatization of public education, and insurgencies attempting to channel the movement toward sectarian ends.

In January 1972, Pastrana brought together leaders of both parties, as well as the key *gremios*, to forge the "pact" of Chicoral. In exchange for paying taxes, landowners were promised easy credit, generous loans, and even more limited land distribution. They were also given a free hand to organize violence against peasant and Leftist leaders, coordinating their efforts with the armed forces. In 1971, ten years after Lleras Restrepo had initiated agrarian reform with Law 135, and five years after he had implemented it as president, roughly 1 per cent of lands that fell under the reform's purview had been expropriated. Landlords with regional power bases formed a solid wall of opposition. Like those of the 1930s, experiments with progressive legislation in the 1960s demonstrated that reform-minded fractions of the elite lacked the capacity to achieve hegemony within the Colombian ruling class. Regional power, based on commerce and landed wealth, stood in the way.

President López Michelsen (1974–78), son of López Pumarejo, had been an intellectual and important political player in his own right for decades, and as founder and leader of the MRL, he had been a fiery rebel against his party during the National Front. Technically, he was the last to serve under the National Front. Through popular caciques like Alfonso Barberena, a leader of squatter settlements in Cali, he courted the urban constituency that had supported Rojas Pinilla. López outlined two Colombias: the first, connected to coffee and manufacturing, included Antioquia, the western Andean departments (Valle, Caldas, Risaralda, Quindío), and the Caribbean port of Barranquilla; it received the bulk of government investment in infrastructure and government services. The 5 per cent of the population that owned more than half the land received half of the national income, and they lived in and governed from the first Colombia. The second, said to cover 70 per cent of national territory, was where blacks, Indians, and frontier settlers lived – the southern and eastern plains and lowlands, and the Pacific and Atlantic coasts. These regions received little investment and had virtually no state presence, electricity, public services, or even minimal infrastructure.

Though coffee prices temporarily reached new highs in the mid-1970s, inflating state budgets, debt service requirements, the near-collapse of traditional industries and elite opposition ensured that López Michelsen's promises of reform and national integration remained unfulfilled. Although López announced his aim of converting Colombia into the "Japan of South America," he was the first president of the National Front to propose neoliberal measures: with Pinochet's Chile as a model, López called for market liberalization, privatization of state enterprises, and fiscal decentralization.[133] Rising entrepreneurs in the marijuana and cocaine businesses helped the change in direction by laundering money legally through the Banco de la República.

General Álvaro Valencia Tovar fought in Korea, at Marquetalia, and Anorí; a follower of Ruíz, he was appointed head of the armed forces under López Michelsen. Like his mentor, he stressed the need for social investment in education, health care, infrastructure, and credit, in areas where communist support predominated.[134] General Luis Camacho

Leyva, a lawyer who saw radical ideas as a cancer in need of extirpation, soon replaced Valencia; this was to be the end of "social investment" as a component of cold war counterinsurgency. Camacho proposed modifying the 1886 Constitution in order to pass a law regarding "thought crimes" (*delitos de opinión*), specifically targeting Left academics and party-affiliated intellectuals. Convinced that most of Colombia's trade unions and universities, as well as community, neighborhood, and peasant organizations were infected by communist propaganda, he publicly accused García Márquez of having guerrilla ties. By 1974, however, ANUC, the main radical opposition movement, had been repressed, co-opted, and rent by Left sectarianism, and the other movements were hardly poised to forge a nationwide coalition for radical change. To the extent that they had survived the first phase (1964–74) at all, rural insurgencies were dormant.

Simmering urban discontent, however, took dramatic form in 1974, when a new group, M-19 – named after the day, 19 April, when the election had been stolen from Rojas Pinilla – announced its appearance by stealing Bolívar's sword from the historical museum in central Bogotá. Composed of middle-class *anapistas* as well as young FARC and PCC dissidents, from the outset, M-19 had a keen sense of how best to exploit the communications media to cultivate the same aura of romantic bravado that had surrounded the urban guerrillas of the Southern Cone, some of whose veterans swelled M-19 ranks. An explicitly national-popular movement, with electoral ambitions in the tradition of Gaitán, M-19's goal was not the overthrow of capitalism or the Colombian state, but the opening up of the existing political system to electoral competition; in this, M-19 was similar to Castro's M-26 movement in pre-revolutionary Cuba.[135] It generated broad though diffuse support among the working and middle classes that had voted for Rojas Pinilla and López Michelsen, and proved far more "popular" than either the FARC or the ELN.

The mid-1970s saw the spread of protests over public services, led by the working class on the urban peripheries, mobilizing through neighborhood associations and cooperatives rather than trade unions. In 1977, the three major trade union confederations staged a *paro cívico*, or civic strike, which General Camacho punished with extreme repression. Thereafter, high unemployment, lower wages, decreased social security and the rise of the "informal sector" – in which more than half the

Colombian proletariat would be toiling by 1985 – further weakened an already divided labor movement.[136]

The crushing of the *paro cívico* set the stage for a widespread crackdown under the next Liberal president, César Turbay Ayala (1978–82). General Camacho was chosen to lead the assault on thousands in the cities targeted as "subversives" by the army, police, intelligence services, and a growing number of paramilitary organizations. Those arrested were tortured, imprisoned, or "disappeared," and death squads like AAA (Anti-Communist Alliance) appeared on the Argentine model.[137] Political violence grew much more intense than it had been during the previous decade, and General Camacho's forces struck particularly hard at M-19. For the first time, counterinsurgent operations affected daily life in the cities, and along with the countries of the Southern Cone, Colombia began to receive attention from the international human rights movement.[138]

The overall climate in the late 1970s and early 1980s, with the urban trade union and civic movements in retreat, and state repression on the rise, was a propitious one for guerrilla growth. There was as yet no discourse of "armed actors of the Left and Right" (as would be pioneered by northern analysts of El Salvador in the 1980s). The brutal repression the Turbay administration meted out, coupled with hopes unleashed by the Nicaraguan revolution and the processes unfolding in El Salvador and Guatemala, gave guerrillas a new lease on life. They argued that Colombia under Turbay was no different from the military juntas of the Southern Cone, while in Nicaragua the Sandinistas had shown that armed struggle was the way to overthrow dictatorship.

Despite the repression directed against it, M-19 initiated its first urban operations in 1978 on General Camacho's watch. The following year, its militants stole 4,000 machine guns from the armory in Bogotá, and, in 1980, occupied the Dominican Embassy with the US envoy inside – operations that were typically flashy and risky, and did not require a broad social base or mobilization.[139] For its part, the EPL dropped Maoism – which had led to innumerable internal splits – in 1980, and made headway in the cattle country of Córdoba and the banana zone of Urabá, which it would later dispute with the FARC.[140]

This latest phase of guerrilla growth, however, took place within a rapidly changing political-economic environment. Restructuring had begun within the fragmented oligarchy during the long stagnation of industrial manufacturing in the 1960s and 1970s. Important factions shifted their investment away from production, toward speculation and the capture of rents. New enclaves, dominated by foreign capital and the production of a single commodity for export, multiplied – the petroleum regions of Arauca and Northern Santander, the coal sector of the Guajira, bananas in Urabá. This latter shift provided the guerrillas with the material basis for expansion.

The marijuana business, initially organized by Peace Corps veterans and quickly taken over by Colombian smugglers, flowered in the Cauca, Cesar, and Magdalena departments, and La Guajira.[141] Construction and banking soared, as a new layer of outlaw rentier capitalists began to acquire the wealth that would allow them to fund the counterinsurgency and enrich themselves through the war economy.[142] The Conservative base continued to shrink.

While fumigation of marijuana in the Cauca and the Sierra Nevada de Santa Marta, and the extradition of leading marijuana traffickers to the USA began under Turbay, cocaine had already replaced marijuana as Colombia's most profitable export commodity. By the early 1980s, narcotics mafiosos entered politics, and "drugs" became the pivot of US-Colombian government relations. The coffee sector was at the beginning of the end of its economic predominance, but the Liberal Party was given a boost with the drug trade, which allowed it to survive, while the Conservative Party all but disappeared. Modernizing technocrats in Bogotá saw their already limited power over the departments diminish further, as new political brokers – more corrupt, cynical, and willing to work with the cocaine mafia than some of the traditional caciques – came to dominate regional and local political landscapes. Provincial clientelism was revamped, and the military and police assumed more prominent roles as the upholders of "public order."

It was within this new context that the ELN, reborn after near annihilation at Anorí, began, from the early 1980s, to target multi-national export enclaves as part of a new "ABC" strategy, based on an analysis of the country's new pattern of resource extraction. They surfaced in the petroleum regions of Arauca and Northern Santander, the El Cerrejón coal-mining zone of the Guajira, and the gold-mining regions of southern Bolívar and northeastern Antioquia, offering a new model of revolution, taken from Central America rather than Cuba. Building on liberation theology, they joined popular movements and worked closely with the more radical sectors of the oil workers' union, USO, as petroleum caught up to coffee as Colombia's leading legitimate export. What the FARC had done in its early days, the ELN did once it dropped Che's *foco* theory and got rid of Fabio Vásquez. They built local power by supporting popular movements.

This move came as a response to armed competition from the Left. At their VII National Congress in 1982, the FARC abandoned its defensive strategy, in theory (they had already done so in practice), to project themselves throughout the national territory – a change symbolized by the initials, EP (Army of the People), added to the group's name. The FARC had already expanded from its bases in Caquetá, Meta, and Putumayo, into the Urabá, the Middle Magdalena, and areas of the southeastern plains – Guaviare, Vichada, and Vaupés – which had indigenous majorities. This was the jump-off point from which, feeding on taxes levied from the country's thriving new cocaine industry, the FARC would become a military enterprise dedicated to territorial expansion and control.

During the National Front, Liberal administrations tried and failed to implement agrarian reform and vanquish armed insurgencies in recently colonized regions. In the mid- to late 1970s, a new wave of radical-popular protest by organized labor, students, and colonizers of the urban frontier, along with a new urban guerrilla insurgency, was rolled back with state-sanctioned terror in the shape of death squads. Designed to deal with the Colombian government's incapacity to stop the spread of insurgency, these were structurally similar to those ravishing the societies of Central America and the Southern Cone. Sanctified by the Catholic Church, anti-communism glued the bipartisan system back together.

In the late 1970s and early 1980s, however, intensified repression diminished state authority and created a climate in which Left insurgencies thrived. Their flourishing, in turn, challenged death squads to consolidate themselves as regional paramilitary forces. Political and criminal violence fed into one another, and homicide became the leading cause of death among males, especially in the urban frontier zones. A major economic shift toward rent, speculation in land and urban real estate, and cocaine exports heralded the death of the coffee republic. By moving the productive base away from manufacturing and coffee exports, toward extractive export enclaves and coca frontiers, the multinational corporations, the narco-bourgeoisie, and technocratic politicians in charge of "modernizing" and "reforming" the Colombian state created the necessary conditions for guerrilla resurgence. Accelerating state and parastate repression provided sufficient conditions.

6

Negotiating the Dirty War, 1982–90

> It is not only a punitive war but a preventive war . . . a dirty war
> . . . It is not only a war against the state or of the state against civil
> society; it is a war of the entire society with itself. It is collective
> suicide.
>
> Gonzalo Sánchez, "La degradación de la guerra" (1991)

Conservative President Belisario Betancur initiated a peace process with
the insurgencies in 1982, out of which a broad electoral Left, tied to the
largest guerrilla insurgency, emerged as the first national-popular expression since *gaitanismo*. In response, regional and local paramilitary
networks defied Bogotá by implementing a "dirty war" – characterized
by high levels of torture, massacre, disappearance, and political murder –
with impunity. When peace negotiations broke down, political violence
against the broad Left – sanctioned by the executive *ex post facto* –
spiraled in proportion to the growing power of cocaine-exporting
entrepreneurs.

I Narco-politics and Paramilitarism

Centered, as the coffee export business had been, on Medellín, cocaine
processing and transport linked the first Colombia of the central and
western highlands to the second Colombia of the eastern lowlands and
Pacific and Atlantic coasts, through new cities like Florencia and
Villavicencio, as well as roads and airports. Medellín thus recovered
its fading industrial glory, becoming the major hub for the one export
commodity Colombians owned and controlled. This was facilitated by
Antioquian migration to South Florida and Jackson Heights, Queens,

which provided the so-called Medellín cartel with distribution net-works.[143]

The growing power of the mafia was first raised in the 1982 elections, when Pablo Escobar and others made inroads into national politics, mainly through the Liberal Party; cocaine had surpassed coffee and earned an estimated 30 per cent of Colombian exports.[144] Escobar became an alternate Liberal deputy in Congress under Alberto Santofimio, one of the most corrupt of the old-style caciques (political bosses).[145] The alliance developed after Escobar had been expelled from "The New Liberalism," led by Luis Carlos Galán and Rodrigo Lara Bonilla, both of whom publicly opposed the growing influence of cocaine entrepreneurs and disputed the legitimacy of caciques within the Liberal Party, like Santofimio.

With their ties to the repressive organs of the state, the Catholic Church, and the two parties, the paramilitaries were able to profit from cocaine exports on a much grander scale than the FARC. They owed this lucrative role to their origin as death squads of the drug cartels and the cattle-ranching anti-communists in the Magdalena Medio Valley. In 1981, traffickers like Escobar, the Ochoas, Carlos Lehder, Victor Carranza, and Gonzalo Rodríguez Gacha, organized MAS, or "Death to Kidnappers," a right-wing paramilitary force dedicated to ridding the region of "subversives." Amplifying the findings of the Prosecutor General's report on MAS, as minister of justice, Lara Bonilla had exposed the connections between active and retired military officials, police, party bosses, cattle ranchers, and narcotraffickers in the formation of MAS.

Like the *pájaros* of the 1950s, MAS's radius of action was at first strictly regional, but it soon branched out. Gonzalo Rodríguez had worked as a lieutenant under Gilberto Molina in the Boyacá emerald mines, where each capo had a rudimentary military apparatus to enforce control over labor and rivals. Rodríguez and Victor Carranza served as a bridge between narco-financed paramilitarism in the Middle Magdalena and the southeastern lowlands of Meta – between the first Colombia and the second. As head of the cattle ranchers' association (FEDEGAN) in Antioquia in 1983, Pedro Juan Moreno Villa defended MAS in a public debate with Lara Bonilla in Puerto Berrío. He built another bridge, stretching from the Magdalena Medio to northeastern Antioquia and Urabá.[146] The regional outlines of a burgeoning paramilitarism were increasingly visible.

Paramilitary leader Carlos Castaño describes a more internationalist formation in his 2001 autobiography, *My Confession*. As an eighteen-year-old former army scout serving in the ranks of MAS, his family sent him to train in Tel Aviv, Israel, in 1983. Detailing how he ordered and participated in massacres of civilians, Castaño insists, "I copied the concept of paramilitary forces from the Israelis." As described below, the lessons learnt in Lebanon, the West Bank, and Gaza were applied in the Magdalena Medio. Castaño worked there under the direction of his drug-trafficking brother, Fidel, a.k.a. "Rambo," a business associate of Pablo Escobar's who would soon devote himself full-time to commanding paramilitary death squads. The "House of Castaño," as Fidel called his regional counterinsurgent movement, had begun its ascent.[147]

In 1984, Escobar ordered the assassination of Lara Bonilla, Betancur's minister of justice. Lara Bonilla's offense had been to resist the influence of the cocaine mafia in Liberal Party politics by demanding that leading traffickers like Escobar be extradited to the USA. The repression of the cocaine business after the killing of Lara Bonilla helped lift it out of the crisis into which it had fallen in 1983. The day of Lara Bonilla's burial, for example, in Calamar (Guaviare) the price of a kilo of coca paste was 200,000 pesos; a week later it cost 800,000 pesos. Narco-investment in land, initially concentrated in the Magdalena Medio Valley, grew rapidly.[148]

Cocaine exporters – who had also invested heavily in finance, construction, and communications – merged with "peasant self-defense" forces in order to protect their newly acquired properties. Drug mafias also aligned themselves with Liberal Party bosses in the provinces, as well as active and retired military and police. Increasingly, they set the parameters for official Colombian politics.[149]

II   "Political Opening"

Supported by "New Liberalism," Conservative President Belisario Betancur (1982–86) made the first attempt to negotiate a cease-fire and a peace agenda with the insurgencies; his Liberal opponent, López Michelsen, had called for their military defeat along Venezuelan lines.[150] Once a follower of Laureano Gómez, but by temperament a loner in the establishment, Betancur was moved by the deteriorating plight of the majority, and aimed to improve it. In 1982, as a first step, he declared an amnesty and freed over a thousand guerrillas and political activists imprisoned under Turbay's draconian "Security Statute." Betancur named social inequality as the culprit of the maladies spawned by the guerrillas, and insisted on executive, rather than legislative, supervision of cease-fire negotiations – although any proposed reforms would have had to go through Congress.

This was the beginning of the period Betancur named the "political opening." Here was a window through which demilitarization of political life and a serious discussion of problems – political exclusion, lack of education, services, and infrastructure, violent dispossession and government neglect in the countryside, unemployment as well as shrinking industrial manufacturing jobs in the cities – could be glimpsed.

The failure of the process is easily explained. With US-funded counterinsurgency wars in Central America moving into critical phases, the international context discouraged a negotiated political solution to Colombia's military conflict. US Ambassador Lewis Tambs coined the term "narco-guerrilla" in 1984, the year the cease-fire was implemented, suggesting that the FARC was criminal rather than political.[151] This came during a period in which, following Ronald Reagan's visit to Bogotá in December 1982, the "war on drugs" became the principle theme of US-Colombian diplomacy. Betancur never had the support of the Colombian Army, which opposed peace negotiations and a political solution on both institutional grounds and cold war principle.[152] Nor did Betancur have strong backing from any faction of the ruling class, and he was dependent on a reluctant Congress for structural change.

Terms relatively favorable to guerrillas bent on joining the formal political arena triggered a reaction from local landed elites, as well as the high command of the Colombian Armed Forces. They fought central government policy using counterinsurgent terror, funded in part by cocaine export revenues – like the Nicaraguan Contra forces fighting to overthrow the national-popular Sandinista regime.[153] In the Magdalena Medio Valley, the eastern plains, northeastern Antioquia, and southern Córdoba, older agrarian elites and the new commercial-financial-industrial cocaine elite established regional beachheads for private armies and landed empires.

As in *la Violencia*, as much as the guerrillas themselves, who were present in the above-named regions, what galled traffickers and traditional landlords alike were processes of self-organization, of which guerrilla insurgency was only one aspect. Self-organization led to escalating demands for redistribution of land, reorientation of credit, and new, state-subsidized technological improvements. Led by the Cattle Ranchers' Association (FEDEGAN), through which paramilitary relations with civil society were organized, landed oligarchs decided the time had come to silence popular demands. This meant death to landless peasants, indebted smallholders, rural proletarians, and the urban movements for homes, services, and public education.

The three insurgencies that entered into negotiations – FARC, EPL, and M-19 – saw the state-sanctioned, public-private repression coming. They exploited contradictions in the peace process to strengthen their own position, calling attention to rising army and paramilitary abuses. Firmly rooted in the savannas of Córdoba and the banana zones of Urabá, the EPL had a major presence in trade unions and community groups. By the time an agreement had been reached in late 1984, the FARC had doubled its number of fronts, from fourteen to twenty-eight. In 1985, hoping a general strike in June would turn into urban insurrection, and complaining of army violations of the cease-fire, M-19 pulled out of the truce. In November their commandos staged a seizure of the Palace of Justice in the center of Bogotá, capturing the Supreme Court within it, and requested negotiations. The Army responded by blasting the building in a tank assault that ended with the slaughter of all those inside. Betancur deferred to the high command; had he demurred, he might have been ousted.[154] The massacre marked the beginning of the end of M-19 as a political-military force.

Within the government, the figure in charge of managing contact with the insurgencies, Jaime Castro Castro, was the political godfather of the Liberal Party cacique, Pablo Emilio Guarín, who supervised anticommunist violence in Puerto Boyacá, a cattle-ranching, paramilitary outpost in the Magdalena Medio Valley. One of the paramilitary training camps there, later staffed by British and Israeli mercenaries, was named after Guarín. During Betancur's peace process, the Magdalena Medio became the territorial heart of the Medellín cartel. "Fumigation of subversion" – through disappearance, displacement, and torture – was carried out. Active and retired military and police officials, and cattle ranchers, coordinated with the XVI Brigade in Puerto Berrío, across the departmental border from Boyacá in Antioquia.[155]

The architect of "peace" in the Magdalena Medio Valley was General

Farauk Yanine Díaz, a School of the Americas graduate who recognized that the key to retaking the area from the FARC and the PCC in the early 1980s was a counterinsurgent "hearts-and-minds" strategy that would integrate the peasantry into the apparatus of repression, whether as informants or combatants.[156] Yanine succeeded where General Ruíz and others had failed in the 1960s and 1970s, so Pablo Guarín considered him a "Super Star . . . within the army."

As the peace process degenerated, developments in the Magdalena Medio met with official approval: in a speech delivered in Puerto Boyacá's Plaza Jorge Eliécer Gaitán, in 1985, President Betancur declared the town a "model of peace" for the rest of the nation. Betancur named General Yanine "the symbol . . . of the resurrection of the Magdalena Medio."[157] Officially, then, peace was understood to mean successful counterinsurgency, based on "political cleansing" and closer collaboration between civilians and the armed forces. Exemplary displays of public-private violence became more common as MAS sowed terror with impunity.[158]

In late 1985, the FARC formed the Patriotic Union (UP) with the PCC, as a civilian front designed to help consolidate a power base within the formal political system prior to laying down arms.[159] The strategy of armed electoral politics carried high risks for UP supporters, especially trade unionists and PCC cadres. But for activists of varying ideological hues committed to progressive social change, the UP became a meeting ground for radicals. A new generation sought to overcome the sectarianism of the 1970s. Most had nothing to do with the FARC or the PCC, so they did not adhere to the *criollo* Leninist doctrine of the "combination of all forms of struggle." UP militants worked for peace, social justice, and "revolutionary change" through the electoral arena. In their commitment to finding a democratic path to revolution, they were similar to the Chilean UP of the 1960s and 1970s – and, if anything, more doomed.

Given the "correlation of forces" (*correlación de fuerzas*), a social democratic electoral politics tied to the nation's largest guerrilla formation resulted in widespread extrajudicial execution of Left politicians and militants, especially in frontier regions. The "orthodox" faction of the FARC understood this and argued for increased militarization.[160] Jacobo Arenas, the only proletarian in the overwhelmingly peasant high command, was the driving force behind the UP. His dream was not, like

Salvador Allende's, to find a parliamentary road to socialism, but rather to build a modern war machine with which to fight the Colombian state and US imperialism.[161] In tragic confirmation of the orthodox position, two years after its foundation, 500 UP militants, including presidential candidate Jaime Pardo Leal – who had won more than any Left candidate in Colombian history in 1986 – had been assassinated.

Pardo realized that the UP and the trade unions had to be independent from the FARC if they were to effect reform. One PCC dissident reflected, "If we didn't embrace democracy and peace in a way that was perfectly open, but rather continued playing on both levels with the UP and the party in the legal sphere and the FARC in the war, we were headed for a holocaust."[162] The orthodox wing of the FARC had no intention of letting go of their "political instrument," and their view gained adherents as bodies piled up. Without analyzing it critically, the FARC justified their existence thereafter by referring to what the victims' families called "political genocide."

Most killings of UP supporters were the responsibility of Rodríguez, Victor Carranza, and the Castaño brothers. Adhering to the declarations of the Colombian Armed Forces, to the effect that the UP was merely the "unarmed wing of the subversion," they declared war without quarter on the party as a way of fighting the FARC. The Castaños, whose father had been kidnapped and murdered by the FARC after the ransom had been paid, had personal reasons for waging their war on civilians. Initially at least, Rodríguez and Carranza, his associate in the emerald mafia, took revenge for a business relationship gone awry.[163] Toward this end, they funded "political cleansing" operations to physically eliminate or forcibly displace those who mobilized for radical democratic reforms.

III   Closure

Within the FARC, only Alfonso Cano, the lone intellectual in Joint Chiefs of Staff, saw how the emerging cocaine export elite had begun to supplant older, beleaguered landed elites in frontier regions through paramilitarism. The narco-paramilitary right congealed as a bloc opposed to Betancur's peace negotiations and democratic opening, considering mass mobilization and progressive electoral politics evidence of an unacceptable degree of insurgent political advance. With factions of the armed forces, ranchers, narcotraffickers, Liberal politicians, and organized death squads coming together against him, Betancur lacked the power to insist on social reform, which would have allowed him to undercut the insurgencies. The process of "political opening" undertaken by the central state was opposed by regional elites, regrouped in defense of "private property" and "public order."

The national political community was not expanded to include Afro-Colombians, indigenous groups, frontier settlers, slum dwellers, feminists, human rights defenders, or green activists working through the UP, much less the Communist Left that had forced the opening. In Urabá and the Chocó, peasant communities, either Afro-Colombian or with a strong Afro-Colombian presence, made the UP their political vehicle; so did mestizo frontier settlers in FARC-controlled areas in the south and southeast (Meta, Caquetá). The insurgencies supported many of the demands of the above-mentioned radical-popular groups. In spite of insurgent efforts to use those struggles for their organizational ends, a broad-based, mostly autonomous mobilization was conflated with "subversion" and suppressed by terror.

The overgrown armed resistance contributed to the weakness and vulnerability of the very movements most likely to bring about changes necessary for a negotiated solution. The *pájaros* had risen again, this time in the guise of MAS and the teenage assassins that made Medellín world-famous. Unlike the *pájaros* of the 1950s and 1960s, *sicarios* in the 1980s and 1990s were hired and protected (or killed) by the cocaine mafia, not the Conservative Party.[164] With Reagan's "war on drugs" – organized out of Miami by then-Vice-President George H.W. Bush in order to fight Left insurgencies – narcotrafficking and extradition would be the main focus of US-Colombian government relations.

Under pressure from Washington, the Barco administration that took over in 1986 – a Liberal landslide on a low vote – pursued the extradition of the Medellín cartel. In an oft-quoted phrase, Escobar declared that he preferred "a tomb in Colombia" to a cell in the USA. He and the group of traffickers he led, known as *los extraditables* ("the ones who can be extradited") depended on informants within the armed forces and intelligence services (DAS, DOC, F-2), and responded by ordering hits on leading judges, politicians, and law-enforcement officials. Yet key ministers, newspapers, and political factions within both parties expressed public support for paramilitary "self-defense" forces, some of them with ongoing ties to the Medellín cartel.

When the paramilitary movement gathered momentum in 1987–88, homicide had already become the leading cause of death among males. Social movements staged massive marches in the cities and the countryside, demanding progressive change, and in some cases moved closer to the guerrilla insurgencies, particularly the FARC and the ELN, who tried to instrumentalize them. The scope of right-wing attacks widened to include students, professors, and distinguished professionals like Dr. Hector Abad Gómez, a human rights activist in the progressive wing of the Liberal Party. As Liberal senator (and perennial presidential candidate) Horacio Serpa pointed out, "In Colombia, thought crimes have become instituted on the ground, and are drastically punished with nothing less than the death penalty."[165] In addition to those whose words and deeds were perceived as "subversive," "disposable people" (*los desechables*) were also targeted. Prostitutes, homosexuals, transvestites, the homeless and mentally ill people, thieves, petty drug dealers, and users were killed in "social cleansing" (*limpieza social*) operations that became generalized in Medellín, Cali, Pereira, Bogotá, and Barranquilla. Active and former police officers were as prominent as traffickers and paramilitaries. Urban violence was dizzyingly plural.

The FARC, meanwhile, had begun its metamorphosis into a tributary statelet in earnest, as kidnapping, extortion, selective assassination, and forced displacement began to figure prominently in zones in which they had recently arrived.[166] The ELN also grew rapidly. By the mid-1980s, extraction of protection rents from the German company contracted to construct the Caño-Limón pipeline in Arauca (with the covert aid of the Kohl government), as well as multinational petroleum companies, gave them the resources needed for expansion. The ELN found supporters and recruits in universities, neighborhood and community organizations, and trade unions. It grew by 500 per cent between 1983 and 1988, and, after the peace process, distinguished itself by its readiness to use terrorist tactics – like kidnapping, car bombings, pipeline and infrastructural sabotage – as a substitute for insurrection.

Although on a lesser scale than the FARC, the ELN could claim a patchwork of regional and local sovereignties. In a covert attack on the ELN, which had not joined the cease-fire, the FARC denounced "kidnapping and all forms of terrorism that threaten human dignity and liberty."[167] In 1987, the FARC and the ELN founded the Simón

Bolívar Guerrilla Coordination (CGSB) with M-19, the EPL, Quintín Lame, and the tiny Trotskyist PRT.[168] Promises of insurgent unity proved illusory, however, as the atmosphere of sectarian competition that had rent the Left since the 1930s lingered.[169] Nevertheless, the CGSB gave voice to a guerrilla movement that, in economic and military terms at least, had become a formidable challenge to the exercise of central government authority. Though we have seen that the FARC had already initiated its organizational transformation into a tributary statelet, it is important to remember how sharply the conflict deteriorated in the late 1980s and 1990s, *after* the peace process had failed.

As part of an official effort to democratize regional politics by loosening the control of the center, in 1988 local elections were instituted for the first time since 1886, with the UP winning 16 mayoral and 256 municipal council races. The unexpected result was to increase violent electoral competition, leading to more "political cleansing" operations. These were meant to deal with the advance of the UP, which threatened to break the bipartisan monopoly at the local level, especially in peripheral or frontier regions. The targets were trade unionists, community organizers, students, professors, indigenous activists, radio journalists, and teachers. As always, above all, they were peasants.

In the banana, logging, and cattle-ranching region of Urabá, massacres started in April 1988 at Mejor Esquina, in which thirty-six peasants died on the orders of Fidel Castaño and Luis Rubio, mayor of Puerto Boyacá.[170] In Remedios, in the gold-mining area of northeastern Antioquia, where *contrachusma* forces had rampaged against *gaitanistas* in the 1950s, the UP won the mayor's office in 1988. Fidel Castaño sent his most methodic killer, a former FARC combatant from the Middle Magdalena, on a homicidal spree the same year.[171] According to an investigation undertaken by the Attorney General's Office, César Pérez, a Liberal Congressman from the neighboring town of Segovia, had been one of the intellectual authors of the crime; paramilitary "self-defense forces" from Puerto Boyacá had also participated.[172] In the Sinú Valley in Córdoba, where *juntas gaitanistas* had also formed after the *Bogotazo*, the EPL and the FARC had thrived alongside vibrant civic, student, and peasant movements. Fidel Castaño bought land in Valencia in 1987, had the UP mayor killed, displaced UP supporters, and from there expanded his political dominion through terror and massacres.[173] Thus the municipalities of Valencia and Tierralta were reconquered from the UP by the Liberal Party.

Liberal Party bosses had most to lose from the rise of the UP, and refused political extinction at the hands of a party founded by the FARC and the PCC. In allying themselves so closely with the counterinsurgency, they repeated the mistakes the Conservative government had made during *la Violencia*. In La Rochela massacre, also in 1989, at the behest of Rodríguez, a team of assassins killed nine judicial investigators looking into a paramilitary massacre committed in the Middle Magdalena. This changed the relationship of the paramilitaries to the central government, which now declared more than 200 of them illegal.

One of Escobar's *sicarios* then assassinated center-Left presidential candidate and leader of the "New Liberalism," Luis Carlos Galán, in August 1989.[174] Like Lara Bonilla, Galán had been intimidated into taking campaign money from Escobar, and then proceeded to fulminate against *traficantes* in favor of extradition to the USA. He was sure to have won in 1990, and his funeral was an occasion of national mourning. Later that year, *sicarios* working for Fidel Castaño and Rodríguez shot down the Left's two presidential candidates: Carlos Pizarro, leader of M-19, and Bernardo Jaramillo of the UP.[175] Here the issue was not money or extradition, but demands Left candidates would make for social justice, democratization of the political system, and structural transformation.

One of the UP's two chief enemies, Gonzalo Rodríguez, died in 1989 after the Cali cartel infiltrated his organization, in league with the same forces that were to bring down Escobar four years later. Fidel Castaño, responsible for the killings of Pizarro and Jaramillo, continued amassing forces, fortunes, and land in Antioquia and Córdoba, while cultivating his taste for modern art in Paris, New York, London, and Madrid. Twenty of the forty-two cadavers from the Puerto Bello (Urabá) massacre in 1990 were found on his ranch in Córdoba, *Las Tangas*, one paramilitary participant testified to torturing victims there all night.[176] In the four regions of Magdalena Medio (dominated by petroleum processing and cattle ranching), northeastern Antioquia (site of Frontino Gold Mining Co. and extensive ranching), southern Córdoba (ranching), and ranching and coca-growing zones in the eastern plains, the regionally based paramilitary Right kept new political expressions from entering formal politics. The foundations of a national-level counterinsurgency movement had been laid down over the corpses of the tortured, massacred, and "disappeared" bodies too numerous to count and too dangerous to investigate.

In the late 1980s, paramilitaries erased the broad Left from the electoral map, reinforced clientelist political controls, and began to acquire vast landholdings, chiefly through massacre and expropriation. They became ever more enmeshed in the cocaine business, which explains, in part, the overlap between politics and organized crime. This process is described in three regions mentioned above in connection with *la Violencia*: the Magdalena Medio Valley, northeastern Antioquia, and Urabá – regional laboratories of what later became a national counter-insurgent project. By the end of the 1980s, it was apparent that, unlike beefed-up insurgencies, cocaine mafias had the capacity to infiltrate the two parties, the police, military, and government intelligence services. Through urban terrorism and assassination of leading judges and politicians, they brought the national government to its knees – a fact not lost on the insurgencies. Even before neoliberal IMF "structural adjustment" further weakened state authority, a new pole of sovereignty shifted the center of the political field to the right.

7

Fragmented Peace, Parcellized Sovereignty, 1990–98

"If we cannot and do not want to modify the circumstances that determine these manifestations of misery, marginalization and despair, then let us eliminate the victims!"

Estanislao Zuleta, in Camacho and Camacho, *Ciudad y Violencia* (1990)

The armed electoral politics that had begun at the end of the "opening" continued after the closure, except that with the elimination of the broad Left, it was the paramilitary Right that was advancing. Great hopes were invested in the progressive 1991 Constitution, but its passage coincided with the highest homicide rate in Colombian history, as larger stretches of territory became disputed among a plurality of what analysts began to call "armed actors." Neoliberal structural adjustment, however, mired urban and rural frontiers in economic crisis. Lack of employment, especially among young males, made the narcotics business the country's main engine of job creation, and kept guerrilla as well as paramilitary recruiting high. Instead of expectations of employment, education, property ownership, and political participation being fulfilled, they were extinguished through violent dispossession. More and more people were "displaced" by civil war, and rather than open up the bipartisan system, demobilization of several smaller guerrilla insurgencies was followed by their physical or political disappearance – or else incorporation into paramilitary forces, which were responsible for the vast majority of massacres and acts of political violence. In spite of local defeats and the massive, almost indiscriminate violence inflicted on civilian supporters, however, insurgent expansion surpassed previous records. What insur-

gencies gained in territorial control and numerical growth, they lost in
political legitimacy, but because of their renewable sources of revenue,
they no longer needed the latter to consolidate themselves organization-
ally and territorially. Hence "fragmented peace" did not lead to the
exercise of greater sovereignty by the central government, but rather to its
opposite: the "parcellization of sovereignty."

I *Neoliberalismo a la Colombiana*

If multiple sovereignties and fractured territories had been a notable
feature of the political landscape in the 1980s, both the insurgencies and
the paramilitaries made qualitative leaps in control over resources,
population, territory, and transport routes during the 1990s. This
was achieved through greater recourse to terror, especially on the
paramilitary side, as counterinsurgency operations were increasingly
privatized and subcontracted. Looking for ways to limit the states' direct
role in repression, modernizing, technocratic elites, linked to US capital
and US institutions of higher learning, actively contributed to this
development. "Democracy promotion" was the name given to the
mix of neoliberal economic policies, political reforms, and the "war
on drugs" that characterized the situation of the post-cold war period.[177]

Harvard-educated Liberal technocrat, César Gaviria, elected in 1990,
convoked a Constituent Assembly to produce a new and more democratic constitution – a second attempt to break the long political
stalemate. The EPL, M-19, Quintín Lame, and PRT guerrilla insurgencies laid down their arms to participate in the process, and as a result
of an upsurge in indigenous mobilization, the resulting 1991 Constitution granted historic rights of territorially based recognition to indigenous peoples.[178] It also attempted to streamline the judiciary and limit the
authority of the executive, introducing proportional representation for
senatorial contests and popular election of departmental governors,
previously appointed by the president. It did nothing to curb arbitrary
military and police powers. Nor did it break the stranglehold of the two-
party system, for that was not its intention.

Gaviria's schemes had little of the moral impulse behind Betancur's
efforts, and yielded bitter fruit. The constitution's rigid provisions for
decentralization, including compulsory central government transfers to
the provinces, strengthened the power of local party bosses, especially

Liberals. This increased political corruption drove the country into fiscal deficit.[179] Decentralization opened a new arena for armed electoral competition, since departmental governors as well as mayors were to be directly elected now. Capitalizing on decentralization, the paramilitaries were now poised to contest insurgent power by taking over regional and local office through the Liberal Party, as Conservatives had done after 1946.

The Liberal Party had regained all the municipalities where the UP had been dominant in the late 1980s, and shared them with the new EPL, which by the mid-1990s was allied with banana owners, the military, the paramilitaries, and Liberal Party bosses. The latter bloc accepted a strong union and EPL political vehicle, as long as they did not dispute the monopoly of regional politics or the concentration of landed wealth.[180] While the Liberal Party had recuperated its position in frontier regions like Urabá, it was increasingly dependent on its alliance with paramilitaries tied to drug trafficking.

Since there was no "political subject" powerful enough to guarantee their implementation, even progressive articles of the 1991 Constitution were dead letters.[181] ADM-19, the legal political entity formed from certain factions of the guerrilla group, faded into insignificance, with many former M-19 militants either assassinated or co-opted into traditional politics. In Urabá, former EPL cadres were integrated into Fidel Castaño's paramilitary "security" apparatus.[182] Sectarian terror on the Left strengthened paramilitary-military positions in key enclaves like Urabá. Between 1991 and 1994, 274 militants of Paz y Libertad (Peace and Liberty), the EPL's political party, were murdered there, mainly by the FARC.[183] After the EPL demobilized in 1991, the FARC fought to occupy its territories to combat their influence in the banana workers' union. This pushed EPL militants into the arms of former enemy, Fidel Castaño, which led to escalating attacks against the union from both sides. The EPL's urban militias murdered 17 PCC activists in December 1993, so the FARC massacred 35 EPL supporters.

Signs of "banditization" and "lumpenization" of armed conflict were unmistakable, as the number of kidnappings and homicides broke world records in the late 1980s and early 1990s, with lines between political and criminal violence increasingly indistinct. In 1991, nearly 4,000 homicides were the cause of 42 per cent of all deaths in Medellín, which had a rate of 325 per 100,000, more than five times higher than non-

Colombian competitors like Rio, and eight times higher than São Paulo.[184] In Latin America, only Peru had witnessed a comparable degree of escalation and degradation of armed conflict, but Peru's economy, like others in the region after the debt crisis of 1982, imploded, while Colombia's economy performed to the standards increasingly set by neoliberal economists.

Gaviria implemented the platform López Michelsen had announced in the 1970s, shifting the economy further toward a model of export agribusiness, capital-intensive manufacturing, rentier speculation in land and urban real estate, and multinational exploitation of petroleum, coal, and gold. Perhaps because of the influx of narco-dollars, in contrast to most of Latin America, economic growth held steady in the 1980s, despite the multiplicity of violences. But Gaviria believed that Colombia had yet to fully absorb the wholesome message of the Washington Consensus. He therefore launched a full-scale neoliberal restructuring program to discipline the middle-class public sector, the organized working class, and the peasantry. With the help of Álvaro Uribe, then a Liberal Party senator, Gaviria slashed the public-sector workforce and set about privatizing health care and social security, establishing the autonomy of the Central Bank, liberalizing the currency and financial sector, reducing tariffs and import quotas, increasing turnover taxes, and flexibilizing labor. Oil exploration contracts were signed with the multi-nationals on even softer terms than before.

One initial effect of neoliberal restructuring was to fuel a narco-financed construction boom, which led to rising inflation. An OECD report on Gaviria's reforms concluded that, of all business sectors, the drug cartels were among the most consistently favorable to neoliberal policies – far more so than other groups of industrialists, landlords, modern exporters or financial services (let alone the armed forces or the Church).[185] They prospered at the expense of food and cash crop producers, who were ruined by low tariffs on imports.

The narco-bourgeoisie helped bury what remained of the national manufacturing industry, since contraband imports through Colón, Panama, proved to be a major money-laundering outlet.[186] By 1988, they accounted for an estimated $1 billion, or 22 per cent of total imports, and enjoyed the support or complicity of customs officials and politicians. Industrial, agrarian, and financial policies were dictated in large measure by the interests of the narco-bourgeoisie, which hastened the reorientation toward rentier capitalism and regional reaction. The economic opening was thus a "*fait accompli* years before it was formally institutionalized" under Gaviria.[187]

Though at first he sought to negotiate with the FARC, by 1992, Gaviria tacked to the right, pursuing a "holistic war" by bombing and occupying its headquarters in May. He negotiated with traffickers, who were given light sentences and immunity from extradition in exchange for confessions and collaboration with the Colombian government. After receiving guarantees that extradition would be prohibited in the new constitution, Escobar surrendered, and built himself a prison ("La Catedral") in 1991, which he staffed with his bodyguards of choice until he escaped in September 1992. By that time, in the grip of paranoia, Escobar had killed many of his closest business associates and buried them in the environs of La Catedral. Survivors united against him with the Cali cartel, the DEA, the CIA, Colombian police and intelligence services, sectors of the army, and DAS, the Colombian equivalent of the CIA, FBI, and Bureau of Customs and Immigration Service.[188]

Escobar's frontal assault on the state forced it to buckle, but power was not so fragmented that a lone warrior-entrepreneur could survive the combined forces of his many enemies. The Cali cartel employed a different strategy than Escobar, which ensured its temporary survival in the war against him. Instead of relying on urban terrorism to fight extradition to the USA as Escobar had done, the Cali cartel infiltrated politics, official institutions, and high society. Their investments were more diversified, their behavior discreet, and, unlike Escobar, they never experimented with anti-imperialist populism, donated housing or dispersed patronage to subaltern clients, or publicly organized regional political movements.[189]

The demise of the Medellín cartel was hastened by Escobar's leanings to the Left, but above all by his inability to keep the Medellín cartel from fracturing under US and Colombian government pressure. Escobar terrorized former associates whom he suspected of working with authorities, and surviving members of the Medellín cartel allied themselves with the Cali cartel and the above-mentioned US and Colombian government agencies. Leading the "Persecuted by Pablo Escobar" group (*los Pépes*), Fidel and Carlos Castaño led terror operations in Medellín against Escobar's family, friends, and employees and their families, and anyone who remained loyal to Escobar was systematically tortured, assassinated, or "disappeared."

When it came to confronting the world's most powerful cocaine baron-cum-*latifundista*, the Colombian government delegated repression to groups who had increasingly taken over the fight against the insurgencies, in coordination with state "security" and intelligence forces. The government's close, counterinsurgent association with organized crime weakened government authority and state sovereignty, and the influence of narcotics in politics did not end with Escobar's death, which merely removed its most visible head.

Thanks to future president Andrés Pastrana and the US government, Liberal Ernesto Samper's presidency (1994–98) was mired in allegations over multimillion dollar contributions to his campaign fund by the Cali cartel. Samper's ties to narcotics led the USA to decertify Colombia in the "war on drugs," dismantle the cartel under US supervision, and even suspend Samper's visa. After the two cartels were dismantled in the mid-1990s, hundreds of smaller, more decentralized syndicates proliferated, and their influence, especially in the Liberal Party, continued unchecked. Colombia had become the second-largest producer of coca leaf following Bolivia, whose production plummeted after 1997, as a result of "Plan Dignity," a US government-sponsored manual eradication program.

As they had during the cold war, the US government and the Colombian military advocated a military solution to Colombia's political conflict. The future of the "war on drugs" had come into view, for in a preview of Plan Colombia, "Operation Splendor" – a fumigation campaign that used glyphosate without the pretense of alternative development – began in Guaviare, Caquetá, and Putumayo in 1995–96. In response, the FARC organized coca growers in 1996–97 to protest fumigation and unfulfilled promises of social investment, demonstrating that they still had strong ties to frontier settlers and coca pickers (*raspachines*). In Putumayo, coca growers were accused of "threatening national security." The idea was to paint the FARC as a "narco-guerrilla," in order to disqualify it as a potential interlocutor in peace negotiations – the tactic first employed by former Ambassador Lewis Tambs. Under this scheme, the FARC would be yet another "cartel," and therefore criminal rather than political.[190] Fumigation would undercut their economic base – or so the theory went.

A severe tightening of monetary policy by the Central Bank, meanwhile, cut into investment, plunging the construction industry into recession. The IMF, summoned in 1998 to sort out Colombia's worst economic crisis since the 1930s, could not have been more sympathetic, its 1999 structural reform program – accompanied by a $1.9 billion loan – making provision for "flexibility" in the face of "events outside government control." Demonstrating the collapse of the productive base in rural areas, the percentage of GDP supplied by agricultural production declined from 43 per cent in 1980 to 13 per cent in 1998, while coffee exports represented only 3 per cent of GNP in 1996. Food imports more than tripled during the 1990s, from $215 million to $715 million.[191] The area under coca cultivation also tripled in the second half of the decade. Poppy production went from zero in 1989 to 61 metric tons in 1998, while Colombia continued to supply 40 per cent of US marijuana imports, as well as 90 per cent of its cocaine.

Given undiminished US consumer demand, the "war on drugs" and neoliberal economic policies contributed to the phenomenal growth of the drug economy, as coca farms became the solution to protracted crisis in the countryside. The failure of the rural cash-crop economies began in the 1960s, and deteriorated with the shift toward agribusiness (soy, cotton, rice) in the 1970s. Political violence intensified after the late 1970s and through the 1980s, and by the 1990s, for frontier settlers in Caquetá, Putumayo, Guaviare, Vichada, Guainía, Vaupés, Sucre, Córdoba, the Chocó, Bolívar, the Santanders – and, to a lesser extent, Antioquia, Huila, Tolima, Cauca, and Meta – coca became the only crop profitable enough to overcome the high transport costs that resulted from the lack of infrastructure.[192] It yielded up to three harvests per year and allowed peasants to recoup investments in one to two years, and by 1998, 80 per cent of the surface area of the FARC-controlled departments of Caquetá, Putumayo, Gauviare, Vichada, Guainía, and Vaupés was covered with it.[193]

The connection between neoliberal agricultural policies – which exacerbated the long-term decline of the countryside – and the spread of illicit crops under insurgent sovereignty could hardly have been more direct. A peasant from southern Bolívar put it succinctly:

> To market one sack of potatoes or yucca costs the peasant between 3 and 5 mil pesos (about $3.50) and is sold in the market between 10 to 12 thousand pesos depending on demand . . . Coca is much easier to plant and process . . . there is no need for transportation

since the narco-traffickers buy in the town at 1,500,000/kilo of paste and export it to other destinations.[194]

The FARC provided a minimal stability for those who might otherwise have been crushed by the liberalization of agriculture and the hurricane of rural violence.

II Insurgent Advance

During the 1990s, the two remaining insurgencies, the FARC and the ELN, exhibited the fundamental paradox of an increasing political delegitimation, accompanied by startling organizational growth. Through the 1970s and 1980s, the guerrillas counted on the sympathy of a substantial minority of Colombia's cultural producers, and maintained links to some unions. In the 1990s they were mostly on their own. In November 1992, a group of the country's leading progressive writers and intellectuals, Gabriel García Márquez among them, wrote an open letter to the FARC and ELN, calling on them to recognize that the wheel of history had turned, to lay down arms, and pursue reform through peaceful means.[195]

The post-cold war conjuncture saw the electoral defeat of the Sandinistas and victory for US-financed neoliberals in Nicaragua, the stalemate of the FMLN in El Salvador, and the decline of the Unión Revolucionaria Nacional Guatemalteca (URNG) – and, not least, the collapse of the Soviet Union. While elsewhere insurgents tended to cut patronage deals with neoliberal governments in the name of electoral democracy, free markets, and globalization, the FARC and the ELN concentrated instead on raising rent extraction and exerting political power at the local level. As in the past, their response to isolation from global and hemispheric trends was to isolate themselves further. The seizure of state power faded from view, but the prospect of controlling the mayor's office and municipal councils appeared.

The FARC's role in taxing the coca paste market placed it in the first links of the chain of commodity circulation that ends in US and European noses. During the long reign of the Medellín and Cali cartels, coca paste production was carried out in the lowland coca-growing regions of Bolivia and Peru – and, to a much lesser extent, FARC territory in southern Colombia – where the coca leaf was made into paste by family farmers, flown to jungle laboratories stocked with chemicals, made into powder cocaine, then transported to storage depots, and moved to US and Colombian cities via cars, trucks, buses, boats, and light and commercial aircraft. Given their occupation of territory outside urban centers, the FARC set the rules of market transactions, but could not directly supervise the production of cocaine and secure distribution networks abroad. Thus, contrary to what the term "narco-guerrilla" suggests, the FARC was nothing like a cartel.

It acted like a statelet, and many narcotraffickers were able to establish working relationships with it, signaling the centrality of the FARC's position in the process of coca paste processing. Without the rise of the coca paste economy in the south and southeast in 1970s and 1980s, the FARC would have had neither a geographically extensive network of semi-dependent clients on the open frontiers, nor a multibillion dollar war chest with which to expand their operations. The Colombian Army would have been faced with the task of taking an isolated region, rather than some 40 per cent of a national territory, divided by three cordilleras and countless rivers.

For many years, the FARC regulated the coca paste market, and without their relative monopoly on violence, the traffickers might have destroyed each other with interminable mini-wars in the jungle. As well as maintaining a reservoir of support in the frontier regions, imposition of law and order allowed the FARC to siphon off fabulous amounts of wealth by levying a tax known as *el gramaje*. This formed part of a pattern of extortion established during *la Violencia*, in which kidnapping, *la vacuna*, and *el boleteo* were employed as fund-raising tactics.

In attempting to answer why, decade after decade, the state failed to break the back of armed resistance, other crucial issues come into play, however: for decades, the FARC had been the armed force of a peasant settlers' movement. However mediated by clientelism and protection rents, its ties to many communities in southern and southeastern regions were long-standing. These were sparsely populated territories that the Colombian government had never administered – no infrastructure or public services; not even party clientelism – but which had undergone successive booms in quinine and rubber. After the 1950s, they filled with people fleeing partisan violence in the highlands. In the mid-1960s, the FARC upheld the radical agrarianism that had marked the 1930s and 1940s. Before the creation of the ANUC in 1968 and the CRIC in 1971, they were the most important force – apart from the PCC, to which they were organically linked – calling on the government to realize promises of land reform and infrastructural development, create credit cooperatives, and provide technical assistance and price supports.

The FARC carried on the legacy of agrarian social democracy inherited from the 1930s and 1940s, combining it with traditions of vengeance characteristic of *la Violencia* of the 1950s and 1960s. This description of FARC politics applies to historic redoubts in Meta, Guaviare, and Caquetá, where FARC sovereignty was most consolidated. This authoritarian social democracy, in the context of the illicit cocaine economy of the 1970s and 1980s, provided a measure of security and a guarantee of the means of livelihood for people who would otherwise have had neither. The absence of the state allowed the FARC to establish vertical networks of patronage and clientelism, but they also built infrastructure (bridges, roads, irrigation), offered or supervised limited basic service provision (water, sewage, health care, education), and governed territory as well as populations.

In the 1980s, genuine sympathy in some of the "liberated zones" gave guerrillas important support. Indeed, in Meta, Guaviare, Caquetá, and Putumayo in the 1980s, hope of agrarian reform had been put to rest; the coca economy was the gold rush of its day. The FARC offered the only protection available against the arbitrary brutality of the traffickers in Meta and Guaviare.[196] Debt-driven mechanisms of labor control, their contracts enforced through assassination – whether inherited from the rubber boom in the southeast or transplanted from the highland emerald mines of Boyacá[197] – cast the FARC as a much-needed arbiter of labor markets.

Until recently, FARC violence unfolded according to predictable, if ruthless, rules that could guarantee "order" and "stability" on the frontier, whereas narco-terror led to "chaos" and "unpredictability," particularly where coca paste prices were concerned. In those frontier regions of the south and southeast colonized by peasants fleeing political violence and agrarian crisis in the highlands, the FARC took up tasks the state had failed to perform. They were the local and regional administration, and by any standard of living memory, even at their worst, they were better than the national government or the traffickers.

Guerrilla financial and territorial expansion was accompanied by higher levels of kidnapping, selective assassination, and car bombing, tactics first routinized by Escobar. As elsewhere, state terror provided the fuel without which insurgent terrorism could not ignite, but in Colombia both were supplemented by the narco-terrorism of the mafia.

Whereas in 1978, the FARC had 17 fronts in peripheral regions, by 1994 it had 105 fronts and operated in 60 per cent of Colombia's 1071 municipalities.[198] Its leadership continued to be dominated by peasant smallholders – a middle-class intellectual and an oligarchic banker provided the only exceptions. Only 10 per cent of the FARC's rank and file were "middle class," 20 per cent were classified as "working class," "students," or "schoolteachers," and the FARC considered 70 per cent of their number to be "peasants" – mainly rural proletarians working as agricultural laborers and/or coca pickers. While 30 to 40 per cent of combatants and mid-level leaders were women, men maintained their grip over the high command.

By 1996, the ELN had between 4,000 and 5,000 combatants, extensive urban militias and support networks, and a presence in 350 municipalities. Protection rents, extortion, bank robbing, and kidnapping provided their chief sources of income.[199] Since they refused to enter the cocaine business, the ELN developed a notable dependence on kidnapping, which earned them the undying enmity of the middle and ruling classes, particularly in the regions. Similar to previous Latin American guerrilla organizations (excepting the FARC and Mexico's EZLN), high-level leadership positions were the preserve of middle-class intellectuals, but ELN front commanders were almost exclusively peasants. Recruits were mainly from smallholding families, but the ELN was also successful in drawing in students and unemployed youth from regional cities like Bucaramanga, Barrancabermeja, Valledupar, and Cúcuta. Outside the Central Committee – which, like the FARC's Estado Mayor, remained a bastion of masculine privilege – 20 per cent of ELN leaders were women, roughly proportional to their numbers in the rank and file.

As they expanded, the FARC and the ELN underwent processes of bureaucratic rationalization – the principal aim of each organization was to consolidate and project itself.[200] Lacking extensive transport and distribution networks, the FARC was in no position to compete with the AUC in international markets. But it offered food, clothing, employment, high-tech weaponry, a cell phone, and a monthly salary to impoverished rural youths who did not want to be government soldiers, peasant soldiers, spies, or paramilitaries. The average age of FARC combatants was nineteen, and they were paid $90 per month.[201]

Another element contributing to guerrilla growth was the breakdown of the rural family as a cultural-economic unit capable of sustaining and protecting its members. Neoliberalism in the midst of escalating warfare had created a generation of rural youth, without future horizons or personal security: the FARC and the ELN offered the possibility of both.[202] Since options were exceedingly limited for young women in the countryside, to a much greater extent than the ELN, the FARC offered opportunities for the exercise of political-military power, especially to those lacking secondary school education. Many uneducated young women in rural areas preferred the guerrillas to the prospect of displacement, unemployment, or prostitution.

In 1996–97, the FARC launched a series of military offensives, unprecedented in scale and scope, as if to dramatize the fragility of state sovereignty: with divisions of between 300 and 1,000 soldiers, they attacked army bases in Las Delicias, Patascoy, San Miguel, Pueres, Caguán, San Juanito, and San José. Doubts about the Colombian Army's ability to respond were well founded. Whereas the average ratio of administrative personnel to soldiers worldwide was 3:1, in Colombia it was 6:1, and the army had little motivation to defeat the guerrillas.[203] Since a larger guerrilla threat, whether real or perceived, meant a larger military budget, minimal regulatory oversight, insulation from public scrutiny, and uncontested institutional centrality, the army was the chief beneficiary of its own ineffectiveness.

As under Turbay (1978–82), during Samper's term the Colombian Armed Forces cast themselves as the last bulwark of the state. Defense expenditures rose sharply after 1995, and by 1998 they were three times higher than in 1994. Yet this failed to generate increased effectiveness in combat – unsurprising, given that most of the money went toward administrative expenses. In 1997, out of a total of 131,000 soldiers, only 22,000, or 20 per cent, were combat-ready. US assistance hit a low from 1991–96, during which time most of the anti-drug "aid" went to the police rather than the military, which had come under fire from human rights organizations in the USA and Europe.

With the military crippled by its own brutality and incompetence, insurgencies policed communities, provided public services and regulatory oversight, determined budget allocations, influenced electoral participation, restricted or permitted geographic mobility, and even arbitrated disputes among neighbors, friends, and family members. Most importantly, the FARC and the ELN collected taxes from narcotraffickers, cattle ranchers, small businessmen and women, and large and medium-sized landowners. Along with kidnapping, tax collection was perhaps the most widely resented of guerrilla tactics. While the AUC charged taxes, most investors, property and business owners preferred to pay high rates of protection rent to fervent defenders of "private property" and "free enterprise." The same was true for foreign corporations, particularly in the petroleum sector, that had to pay high rents and were often subject to peasant movement-insurgent demands for social investment in health care, education, and infrastructure. In Casanare and Arauca, for example, the insurgencies forced British Petroleum to invest in schools, vocational training, and local development projects.

Petroleum companies and other multinational corporations preferred to invest in lobbying the US government for increased military aid to Colombia rather than continue funding the insurgencies. Occidental and B.P.-Amaco, the two largest players in the Colombian oil market, teamed up with other energy firms, including Enron, to form the US-Colombia business partnership in Washington. Their financial support for the military and paramilitaries was documented. Given that private property rights were contested in much of Colombia, it was not surprising that foreign corporations paid protection money to paramilitaries as a "capitalist insurance policy."[204]

III Counter-Advance

Though guerrilla expansion in the 1990s was exceptional, paramilitary advance was even more impressive. As we have seen, guerrilla exactions, and the threat they posed to the property and security of elites, explained part of the paramilitary reaction, which began as a political response to Betancur's peace process in 1982–83, grew in the fight to prevent the democratization of political decentralization under Barco in 1987–88, and contracted after guerrilla demobilization and the Constituent Assembly under Gaviria in 1991–92. It surged again under Samper, though at a lesser pace than it had under Barco. Since insurgencies made few political – as opposed to territorial and military – advances under Samper, there was little impulse to prioritize expansion and political integration.

When Fidel Castaño disappeared in 1994, Carlos Castaño took over the family business, founding the ACCU (Peasant Self-Defense Forces of Córdoba and Urabá) that year. During Álvaro Uribe Vélez's term as governor of Antioquia, from 1995 to 1997, the ACCU took Urabá's strategic corridor to the Caribbean from the FARC, cementing alliances with the military and other regional paramilitary blocs under ACCU leadership.[205] Flush with victory in Urabá, AUC chief Carlos Castaño predicted there would be many, many massacres on the model of Mapiripán, Meta.[206]

Located in the heart of the FARC territory, at the crossroads of the coca economy, near the border of Meta and Guaviare, Mapiripán was literally a case of deaths foretold. On 12 July 1997, two charter flights of fifty paramilitary "soldiers" were flown from Urabá into the airport located in San José de Guaviare. The airport was under military control, next to the counter-narcotics base of the Joaquín Paris Battalion—at that time the only base in Colombia from which US-led fumigation operations were being conducted. With the sergeant in charge of airport security and an army intelligence official present, paramilitaries unloaded guns, uniforms, and communications equipment, which soldiers then helped load onto trucks that would take them to boats. To get to Mapiripán from San José by river, they passed by the checkpoint of the Colombian Army's Special Training School at Barracón, located on an island just downstream from San José.

Trainers from the US 7th Special Forces Group were helping to instruct their Colombian counterparts from the 2nd Mobile Brigade in military planning. The paramilitary presence, reinforced with 180 locally recruited troops, went "undetected" because Barracón's Commander, Colonel Lino Sánchez, a School of the Americas graduate, had assisted in planning the massacre. Upon arriving in Mapiripán, paramilitaries embarked on five days of torture and murder, taking victims from their list of "guerrilla supporters" to the town's slaughterhouse. There, amidst screams and cries for help heard throughout the town, they were disemboweled so that they would not float after being dumped in the river. Judge Leonardo Iván Cortés, who later fled the country under death threats, wrote letters and made phone calls to the military. Colonel Hernán Orozco claimed he had no troops available, but promised to send word to his superior, General Uscátegui, who was in charge of the VII Brigade in Meta and Guaviare, headquartered in Villavicencio. As usual, neither the police nor the military arrived until after the bloodshed had abated.[207]

Ironically echoing Che Guevara's call for "many Vietnams," Carlos Castaño's dark prophecy came true, as paramilitary massacres mushroomed from 286 in 1997 to 403 in 1999, mainly in areas of land concentration and class differentiation.[208] After the push into Meta and Guaviare in 1997, the AUC moved into Northern Santander, Santander, southern Sucre, and the part of Urabá in the Chocó. The curve of paramilitary growth overlapped closely with that of hectares devoted to coca cultivation, for under the direction of Carlos Castaño and Salvatore Mancuso, the AUC vastly expanded its control over the process of cocaine production, transport, and distribution. The number of massacres – most, though not all, committed by paramilitaries working in tandem with or clearing a path for the military – quadrupled during the mid- to late 1990s.[209]

Developments in Urabá illustrate how agro-industrial development, extensive cattle ranching, cocaine production, and transport went hand in hand with a paramilitary project of regional territorial conquest, which reinforced patterns of racial domination and class exploitation derived from colonialism. As governor of Antioquia, Uribe had set about legalizing and regulating anti-guerrilla militias – Convivirs, or Rural Vigilance Cooperatives. The brainchild of Rafael Pardo, Gaviria's minister of defense, Convivirs were structurally similar to the Peruvian *rondas campesinas*, or the Guatemalan Civil Defense Patrols of the 1980s. They were modeled after a program in Córdoba that had grouped 950 cattle ranches into a network connected by a technologically sophisticated communications network. Linked to both General Camacho's AAA and MAS, General Harold Bedoya headed the Colombian Armed Forces from 1994 until 1997, and supported the Convivirs vociferously. For Bedoya, civilian collaboration with the armed forces was compulsory. The Magdalena Medio Valley was Bedoya's referent.[210]

During the two years Uribe served as governor of Antioquia, Convivirs displaced some 200,000 peasants, mainly from Urabá. Antioquia accounted for 18 per cent of displaced people nationwide, more than any other department, and the Conservative Antioquian senator, Fabio Valencia Cossio, accused Uribe of "sponsoring paramilitaries" that had helped contribute to an almost 400 per cent increase in the homicide rate.[211] In neighboring Córdoba, where paramilitary chieftain Salvatore Mancuso ran a Convivir unit, Convivirs displaced 10 per cent of the population in 1995 alone.

Under state-of-siege provisions, and with President Samper's approval, Uribe created "Zones of Public Order," under the command of General Rito Alejo del Río – another MAS veteran, and Bedoya protégé – and the XVII Brigade in 1996. General Bedoya declared that those who opposed the zones "defend the interests of narco-traffickers or subversives."[212] According to Colonel Carlos Velásquez, who served under him, General del Río's first move was to remove troops from areas where they were protecting civilians from paramilitary incursions.[213] In the four municipalities in the banana axis, the homicide rate was 500 per 100,000, as opposed to 60 per 100,000 nationwide (in the USA, it was 8 per 100,000). Although the total number of homicides in Urabá's banana zone was high before Uribe took over as governor (400 in 1994), it got worse during his term: in 1995, it doubled to 800; in 1996, 1,200; and in 1997, 700. In 1998, the year after Uribe's departure, it dipped to 300.[214]

In the 1950s and 1960s, General Ruíz had been emphatic about the importance of social investment, but in the neoliberal era, that variable was dropped from the counterinsurgent equation. In line with National Security Doctrine, when Plan Cóndor cast its long and bloody shadow over South America in the 1970s, General Camacho created and promoted paramilitary groups under Turbay. The goal had been to reduce the level of human rights violations attributable to the Colombian police and armed forces, while wiping out "the subversion." Paramilitary presence spread incrementally under Turbay, Betancur, Barco, and Gaviria, but given the regional fragmentation of power, counterinsurgents were unable to function as a unified force until the mid-1990s. Thereafter, they became more effective in generating employment while redistributing wealth, political power, and property toward the light-skinned top of the social pyramid.

The regional state was prepared to look for ways to "legalize and regulate" anti-guerrilla militias, further eroding the line separating politics from organized crime. Agencies of state repression had committed upwards of 75 per cent of human rights violations through the late 1980s, but by the late 1990s the AUC was responsible for roughly the same percentage, while the army and police committed a mere 5 per cent of total violations.[215] From 1997 to 2000, paramilitary numbers doubled.

This was how privatized, subcontracted counterinsurgency was supposed to work. Amnesty International, America's Watch, and other human rights groups signaled close connections between Convivirs and paramilitaries. The organic unity between the two was manifest: at the end of 1999, when the Constitutional Court banned the Convivirs for numerous massacres of unarmed civilians, their foot soldiers simply passed into the ranks of the AUC.

Victims were anything but passive. Backed by US human rights groups, like the Peace Brigades International, Colombia Support Network, and the Fellowship of Reconciliation, a "peace community" movement gathered steam in Urabá in the mid-1990s.[216] Political violence against civilians reached shocking levels, even by Colombian standards, which were then among the highest in the world. After the ACCU displaced some 15,000 people from the area around the country seat of Apartadó, with the help of the Catholic Diocese and Colombian NGOs, peasants who refused to be dispossessed founded the Peace Community of San José de Apartadó (pop. 1,200) in March 1997. Peace communities like San José were established as multi-ethnic neutral zones outside the larger war system. Setbacks, particularly the assassination of leaders, massacres, and economic blockades, did not stop communities from working to live in peace, without having to pay tribute to military authority. Gloria Cuartas won international recognition for her efforts to protect the civilian population as mayor of Apartadó, and she accused government soldiers of permitting the ACCU to decapitate a child, César Agusto Rivera, in front of her and 100 children, during the inauguration of "Peace Week" in August 1996. At a meeting of departmental officials, Uribe's secretary of government, Juan Moreno, publicly accused Cuartas of being a FARC spokeswoman, while General del Río sued her for defamation.[217]

In the face of massive repression from the paramilitary right and insurgent Left, peace communities like San José de Apartadó fought for a different vision of sovereignty, as peace and self-determination, and for collective social rights as well as individual political and civil rights. But by the late twentieth century, organized right-wing repression, and the military hypertrophy of the armed Left, led to the relative weakness and fragmentation of Colombia's radical-popular movements.

Political decentralization and delegation of repression – key features of the 1990s – weakened and delegitimized the central government authority it was supposed to support. A pet project of the World Bank, decentralization meant that both state governors and mayors were popularly elected for the first time since 1886, but this only exacerbated the lack of central government authority and spurred the retrenchment of regionally based narco-landlord power in the Liberal Party.

Using terror tactics pioneered in the 1950s, this bloc successfully insulated electoral politics from the broad Left challenge. This helped insurgencies accelerate the trend toward territorial expansion in the first half of the 1990s, while previously disparate regional paramilitary groups united in a national umbrella organization in the second half. US-sponsored chemical warfare – the spraying of insurgent-held areas in the southeast with Monsanto's Round-Up Ultra (glyphosate) – had returned, and US government pressure on nearly all aspects of policy increased alongside funding for the "war on drugs." The US and Colombian governments turned a blind eye to the increasing reach of the paramilitaries, focusing instead on eliminating Left insurgencies by strengthening the Colombian military and police.

8

Involution, 1998–2002

War is paid for in land . . . Our history is one of incessant
displacement.

Alfredo Molano, *Los Desterrados* (2002)

Since the late 1990s, the widening of the counterinsurgency war in the
jungles and plains of the south and southeast has formed the axis of
public policy, as military and paramilitary expansion accompanied peace
negotiations with the FARC. In 1998, the creation of a Switzerland-sized
"demilitarized zone" in the south, officially governed by the country's
largest insurgency, raised hackles in Colombian regions, as well as in
Washington. Under Presidents Clinton and George W. Bush, the US
and Colombian governments implemented Plan Colombia, a five-year,
$4 billion "aid" package, 80 per cent of it earmarked for the Colombian
police and military. The stated goal of Plan Colombia was to cut
narcotics production by half in six years, and to conquer the 40 per
cent of national territory held by insurgents.

I Electoral Pacts, Elusive Peace

Pacts for peace with the insurgencies determined the outcome of the 1998
elections, as did pacts with paramilitary counterinsurgents in 2002.
Divergent campaign strategies and political programs shared the common
goal of strengthening central government authority, but highlighted the
salience of new forms of armed clientelism instead. The shift in policy –
from peace with the insurgency to peace with the paramilitaries – led to the
end of the bipartisan monopoly on political representation, and coincided
with deepening US government involvement in Colombia's civil war.

In spite of their exclusion from formal politics, Left insurgencies and the right-wing counterinsurgency helped determine electoral outcomes at the national as well as local and regional levels – mayors, the city councilors, municipal officials, departmental governors, departmental and congressional representatives, and senators. When Conservative Andrés Pastrana was elected president (1998–2002), many agreed that the promise of peace negotiations with the FARC had netted him victory, but it was quickly forgotten that Liberal Horacio Serpa also campaigned on a "peace" platform.

Serpa promised to negotiate with the ELN rather than the FARC. Going against the counterinsurgent grain, both candidates recognized the political character of the guerrillas, as did more perceptive critics on the Left: "They are not simply bandits, terrorists, or narco-guerrillas, but rebels with ideology, resources, and specific objectives against the existing order."[218] Agrarian reform, for example, was a non-negotiable demand. So was the reorientation of the economy, away from the neoliberal export model, toward a nationally oriented developmentalism, more or less modeled on Sweden. The state was an enemy with which it was possible, at least in theory, to negotiate. But insofar as the FARC considered invalid the distinction between paramilitaries and the Colombian military, paramilitary expansion and peace negotiations were incompatible. The FARC's ideology would be best described as ossified, militaristic Marxism mixed with progressive creole liberalism. It was the authoritarian social democracy proper to a tributary statelet based in the countryside and small towns.

Unlike Pastrana and the FARC, Serpa and the ELN had promised to broaden the discussion about war, peace, and social change, to include "civil society," a concept in which the FARC did not believe, since they had a Manichean, "friend-enemy" understanding of politics that did not admit the possibility of autonomy.[219] Perhaps unrealistically, agribusinessmen and cattle ranchers, as well as peasants, trade unionists, students, community organizations, the unemployed and middle-class professionals, were to bring forward demands and proposals. The ELN asked that several municipalities in the Magdalena Medio be "demilitarized" (officially recognized as ELN territory), in order to conduct negotiations away from the battlefield. The agreement, forged in Mainz, Germany, in July 1998, was designed to lead to debate and discussion about investment and regional development in the Middle Magdalena Valley.

Predictably, the peace process with the ELN was sabotaged by the AUC. It would have favored medium and small peasant producers, demonstrating the possibility of regional agreements for political and social incorporation – supported by the "international community" – that included investment in health, education, and infrastructure. It represented an opportunity to implement a small-scale agrarian reform that dealt not only with land distribution and titles, but credit, distribution, and transport, and might have proved to skeptics that progressive change was possible at the local and regional levels. But the AUC, in a repeat of the experience of Puerto Boyacá under Betancur, mobilized clients in opposition, and blocked transport routes through the country's chief arteries.[220] Since Serpa lost, the proposal was dropped, and Pastrana favored the "fragmented peace" that prevailed under Gaviria, negotiating directly with the FARC. This was a prolongation of war and neoliberal technocratic rule.

Yet Pastrana withdrew the armed forces from a demilitarized zone of some 16,200 hectares in the Caguán region of Caquetá in November 1998, as a preliminary concession to the FARC. In effect, he recognized their sovereignty over the region, which was logical given that the FARC was the only group ever to have administered the territory. By the end of 1999, Pastrana and the FARC approved a twelve-point program for negotiation, including issues of agrarian reform, human rights, natural resources, and socioeconomic restructuring. But Pastrana lacked the power, or the will, to deliver on reforms – other than neoliberal austerity measures demanded by the IMF in exchange for a $1.9 billion loan. Despite occasional high points – one came in early 2000, when FARC representatives and Colombian government officials went on a "learning tour" of European capitals; another in June 2001, when the FARC released 363 captured police and soldiers in exchange for 11 (not, as promised, 50) of their own – the peace process was stillborn. The FARC withdrew from preliminary negotiations in late 1999 and 2000, due to the government's unwillingness or inability to rein in the military and the mushrooming paramilitary forces. They then used the demilitarized zone to hold a pool of kidnap victims numbering several thousand, and prepare for future battles.

On 20 February 2002, under intense pressure from the military, the politically ascendant reactionary bloc, and the media, Pastrana ordered the Colombian armed forces to retake the FARC's demilitarized zone.

He did so with international backing, and the attacks of September 11 helped to delegitimize the FARC at home and abroad. Because of their tactics and their misunderstanding of the role of public relations in contemporary politics, they lost what little chance for political legitimacy the peace process had offered. In spite of Pastrana's unpopularity when he left office, much of the urban and small-town population was convinced that the country's problem was "insecurity" – kidnapping, drug trafficking, extortion, terrorism. The insurgencies, especially the FARC, were generally held responsible.

Pastrana set the stage for Uribe, accomplishing what no other president had: Tirofijo, the FARC's legendary septuagenarian leader, had become the only politician more unpopular than Pastrana himself. Thus, by raising kidnapping, extortion, and selective assassination to new, atrocious proportions, in 2001–2, the FARC – and, to a much lesser extent, the ELN – helped the rise of a "strong-hand" ruler like Uribe. Between 1997 and 2001, the FARC kidnapped 3,343 civilians and the ELN, 3,412. Kidnapping was the most important source of financing for the ELN, and the second-most important for the FARC.[221] The FARC's tactics, represented for many by the cylinder bombing of a church in Bojayá, Antioquia, in April 2002 – which incinerated 119 Afro-Colombian men, women, and children – made them far more disreputable than they had ever been before.

The only group of the ruling class that supported the peace process with the FARC was the "*cacaos*," a group of financial-industrial-media conglomerates, which, though economically dominant in the 1990s, was unable to lead the ruling class as a whole. Economic preeminence did not translate into increased political clout, for the peace process generated vehement repudiation from the Liberal Party and groups opposed to peace negotiations under Betancur. Landlords, whose class composition changed as narcotrafficking speculators swelled their ranks, behaved as before, using violence to concentrate land and dominate local and regional politics. Working with the Liberal Party, traditional landed elites fused parvenu drug merchants, agribusiness enterprises, and the military and police.

Politically, this reactionary bloc was much stronger than the *cacaos*.[222] Thus the FARC can hardly be blamed for skepticism, even cynicism. Colombian history taught them that "negotiation" meant preparation for war, and that "amnesty" was a synonym for extrajudicial execution.

Throughout Pastrana's presidency, the AUC, allied with cattle ranchers, agro-exporters, factions of the military and police, business and industrial groups, influential sectors of the Catholic Church and the Liberal Party, massacred the social base of the FARC and the ELN in record numbers.[223] In many ways it was a repeat, in a major key, of the war orchestrated during the peace process with Betancur, yet by now the US government's involvement was much greater, as was the reach of the paramilitaries.

II   Plan Colombia

With popular protest, mobilization, and center-Left electoral victories spreading in the Andes after 2000, Colombia became an increasingly geostrategic ally for the US government. Under Presidents Clinton and George W. Bush, the US and Colombian governments implemented Plan Colombia, ostensibly designed to combat the explosion of narcotics production – despite the demise of the Cali cartel in 1996, in the late 1990s, "the business" (*el negocio*) was better organized than ever. After the downfall of the country's two major cartels, delegation of repression and political decentralization was accompanied by the decentralization of the narcotics industry. By 1999, sales of Colombian cocaine, marijuana, and heroin generated an estimated $46 billion in revenues, of which Colombia's share was $3.5 billion, a sum nearly equivalent to the $3.9 billion from petroleum, Colombia's chief export. This was due in part to alliances formed between traffickers and the AUC – or, less often, the FARC – that were difficult for uncorrupted officials to dismantle.

The FARC earned an estimated $900 million in 1999, and in 2000, total coca production was up to 136,200 hectares, 70 per cent of it in the FARC heartlands of Guaviare, Caquetá, and Putumayo.[224] Retired General Barry McCaffrey, President Clinton's "drug czar" and former head of US Southern Command, urged US legislators to embrace the war on "narco-terrorism" – the idea being that since the FARC functioned like a cartel, to fight the "narco-terrorist" FARC was to fight the "war on drugs."[225] In theory, helicopters, tanks, planes, radar, satellite communications, and state-of-the-art training were to be used only to fight the "war on drugs," but in practice they would be used to strike at the FARC and its war economy. This was in keeping with recommendations from a RAND report which urged the defeat, as opposed to mere containment, of insurgencies, citing the examples of Peruvian *rondas campesinas* and Guatemalan *guardias civiles* in support of a more straightforward military-paramilitary counterinsurgent strategy.[226] Another RAND report mentioned the example of El Salvador in the 1980s as a model for what US policy toward Colombia should look like.[227]

Though the "war on drugs" was folded into the "war on drugs and terror," beginning in 2002, in Colombia, too, there was a story about oil:

> After Venezuela and Mexico, Colombia is the third largest source of Latin American oil for the United States – accounting for some 3 per cent of US consumption – even though most of the country's oil resources have remained uncharted so far . . . We might add that, contrary to popular perceptions, the US imports for its domestic consumption more oil from Latin America than from the Middle East; and that Colombia shares with Venezuela and Ecuador the Venezuela-Orinoco belt which is widely suspected of having perhaps the largest pool of hydrocarbons in the world. The future of US-Venezuelan relations, hence of Venezuelan oil for US consumption, is uncertain. The importance of Colombian supplies, present and future, rises proportionately.[228]

At stake, then, was control of Colombia's future oil reserves – thought to be located in FARC territory – and the containment of Hugo Chávez's Bolivarian revolution. Colombia received aid far beyond what any government outside the main foci of the new, or – in the case of the occupied territories in the West Bank and East Jerusalem – the old, colonial wars.[229]

Plan Colombia called for a "push into the south," meaning Putumayo and Caquetá, coca-growing areas under FARC control; "anti-drug aid" would therefore be used for counterinsurgency. John Kerry argued from the Senate floor that although "the line between counternarcotics and counterinsurgency is not at all clear in Colombia," the US government "cannot let this stop . . . extension of aid."[230] "Aid" to the Colombian Armed Forces and police had doubled each year from late 1997 to 2000, and although Plan Colombia had been discussed as early as mid-1998, it did not become a priority for the Republican-led US Congress until mid-1999. The FARC's Bloque Oriental caused an international outcry when it killed three North American indigenous rights activists working with the U'wa indigenous people to keep Occidental out of U'wa territory.[231] Soon after, the Colombian minister of defense, no friend of the U'wa, resigned in protest against ongoing peace negotiations with the FARC.

In August, General McCaffrey visited Bogotá with Undersecretary of State Thomas Pickering, urging Pastrana to craft a proposal designed to strengthen the Colombian Armed Forces, deepen the "war on drugs," and stop economic hemorrhaging that had begun in 1998. Less than two months later, Plan Colombia was circulating in English, and by July 2000 it had been signed into law – in Washington rather than Bogotá. President Clinton breezily waived human rights provisions (the Leahy Amendment) in late August 2000, giving a tacit nod to military-paramilitary collaboration, and opening the door to the disbursement of $1.3 billion in "aid," 80 per cent of it to the military and police. As Plan Colombia was set to go into effect, the AUC announced their arrival in Putumayo, with "political cleansings" and massacres. Their mission, evidently, was to clear a path for rapid military advance, which duly materialized in December 2000 in the form a 1,000-man counter-narcotics battalion. This was designed to secure the coca fields long enough for Colombian pilots and US mercenaries to fumigate them. Within a year, the AUC had become the lords of cocaine in Putumayo.[232] Under Plan Colombia, they then moved into the neighboring departments of Nariño and Caquetá, which soon became two of the country's most conflictive and coca-ridden departments.

Plan Colombia succeeded in professionalizing the Colombian Armed Forces and police, and fumigating large swaths of the countryside, but did not weaken the insurgencies or dent the narcotics business. And by strengthening the AUC's principal allies in the military and police, Plan Colombia strengthened the paramilitaries. It did not target the many areas, especially in the north, where the AUC supervised coca cultivation, secured airstrips, and provided security for transportation. In a public interview in 2000, Carlos Castaño estimated that 70 per cent of the AUC's revenues came from the narcotics business. Pastrana's Ambassador to Washington, Luis Alberto Moreno, put the figure at 75 per cent. Plan Colombia did not put a stop to this pattern; if anything, it deepened it.

Often working or coordinating with the Colombian military, paramilitaries increased massacres, expropriation, and displacement, from 1998 until they entered into negotiations in 2002, at which point they stopped headline-grabbing violence, without renouncing terror as their tactic of choice, or narcotics trafficking and expropriation as sources of power. The increase in guerrilla kidnappings paralleled the rise of paramilitary massacres, but the latter affected mainly peasant small-holders, frontier settlers, rural laborers, and Afro-Colombian and in-digenous communities, while the former was aimed chiefly at the middle class and propertied.

III   Family Ties

In taking aim at kidnapping, the AUC and its preferred candidate, Álvaro Uribe Vélez, played on the fears of urban and rural property owners. To these groups, they offered an illusory "security" from insurgent threats; to unemployed youth in the city and country, they provided jobs in the flourishing private security business. Like Castaño's, Uribe's father had been murdered by the FARC. Ghosts from *la Violencia* reappeared: the overcoming of personal trauma and the restoration of family honor through counterinsurgent warfare were distinguishing features of Uribe and Castaño's political personae.[233] These personal histories were mobilized to powerful rhetorical effect – most middle- and ruling-class people identified with this kind of suffering, as did the families of soldiers, policemen, and suspected or actual paramilitaries.

Support for Uribe and a "peace process" with the AUC was therefore widespread, and Uribe was elected on a simple, clear-cut program: there would be no more attempts to treat with subversion. The solution to the insurgencies was to eliminate them. The most important lobbies behind this reverse course were the Liberal Party, the military high command, multinational banana companies, palm oil processors, flower magnates, narco-barons, and cattle ranchers. Even as they funded the partially privatized counterinsurgency, they called for increased state-led violence against the insurgencies, broadly defined to include anyone working for progressive social change.[234] Their candidate in the 2002 election was Álvaro Uribe: he was, in the words of Carlos Castaño, "the man closest to our philosophy."

The core of that philosophy stemmed from a particular view of the role of civilians in the conflict. As Castaño put it, "In war, unarmed civilian is a relative term. Two thirds of the guerrillas are unarmed, act like civilians, and collaborate with the guerrillas."[235] At the heart of

Uribe's "democratic security" policies was the notion that the state needed citizens to collaborate with the armed forces. Uribe has said, "In democratic societies there is no citizen neutrality in the face of crime. There is no distinction between police and citizens." Compare this statement to General Bedoya's: "Concerning the criminals, no one can be neutral . . . Neutrality is not possible. You are with the terrorists or you are against them."[236] Bedoya's view, we note, was articulated before 11 September 2001. Much like the Bush administration in Washington, Uribe's is a semi-authoritarian form of parliamentary government that does not respect individual rights or international law.

This represented an extension of the cold war. In building a nation-wide network of spies, "peasant soldiers," and "forest guard" families, Uribe followed ideas first articulated and practiced by General Ruíz in the 1960s; from the 1970s through the 1990s, Generals Yanine, Camacho, Bedoya, and del Río encarnated aspects of this philosophy. General Yanine and Pablo Guarín first put it into practice in the Magdalena Medio in the early 1980s. It developed further in north-eastern Antioquia and southern Córdoba in 1987–90, under Fidel Castaño, and Carlos Castaño and General del Río perfected it in Urabá when Uribe was governor of Antioquia. Civilians needed to collaborate with the armed forces, especially in intelligence gathering – or else. Uribe's objective of recruiting 1 million paid informers was rapidly surpassed: 1,500,000 more than planned had signed up by August 2004. Uribe's army of 20,000 "peasant soldiers" (*soldados campesinos*) relied on kinship and friendship networks for intelligence, which meant that for every peasant soldier, there were perhaps four unpaid informers. The same was true of the 36,500 "forest guard" families; all along the Atlantic coast, these were dominated by the AUC.

Uribe's first steps as president were to declare a State of Emergency on 11 August – a mere four days after his inauguration ceremony was met with FARC mortar fire – and open "negotiations" with the ACCU (the leading bloc of the AUC). In order to do so, he repealed Law 418 of 1997, which stipulated that the government could not sign accords or dialogue with a group lacking political status, and replaced it with Law 782, which removed the stipulation.[237] Uribe also levied a special tax to fund the war effort, supplementing Plan Colombia. US troops, US aircraft and US surveillance technology operated in support – or guidance – of the "bandit-extermination" campaigns under way in petroleum-rich Arauca, Sucre/Bolívar, and the coca-growing regions of the south and southeast.

The Justice and Peace Law passed in June 2005 gave near-impunity to demobilized paramilitaries (see Chapter 9, below), but raised unanswered questions about Uribe's family history. Congressman Gustavo Petro, a former M-19 militant, was one of a number of opposition politicians who denounced Uribe's close ties to narco-paramilitarism. These allegations surfaced as the AUC prepared to enter formal politics in the 2006 election cycle, with assets and armies intact. When Petro pointed out that one of Uribe's brothers and two second cousins had much to gain from the new legislation, the *Miami Herald* echoed the allegations, mentioning Uribe's father in connection with the Ochoas and Pablo Escobar. Specific properties – one of which, "La Carolina," the president co-owned with the brother in question – and paramilitary groups ("The Twelve Apostles," "The R's") were named in connection with the allegations.[238]

While circumstantial, the evidence is suggestive. Uribe's father, Alberto Uribe Sierra, had been languishing in debt in the middle-class Medellín neighborhood of Laureles, in the mid-1970s, when a strange reversal of fortune catapulted him to wealth and influence as political broker, real-estate intermediary, and "recognized trafficker."[239] He boasted extensive cattle ranches in the savannas of northern Antioquia and southern Córdoba, and was part of a group of Antioquian narco-speculators who bought land on the cheap in areas where the FARC and the EPL were active.

Uribe Sierra was connected by marriage to the Ochoas, a ruling Antioquian family that joined the upwardly mobile mafiosos to form the Medellín cartel (and MAS); when Pablo Escobar launched his "Medellín without Slums" campaign in 1982, Uribe Sierra organized a fund-raising horse race to help out. Uribe *fils* was first appointed to his post as mayor of Medellín in 1982, as a favor to Uribe Sierra for having helped finance Belisario Betancur's campaign. He was quickly removed by the then-governor of Antioquia.

During Uribe's brief tenure, traffickers referred to Medellín as "the sanctuary." It has been suggested that his removal came after his conspicuous attendance at a meeting of the region's drug cartel at Escobar's hacienda, located in the Magdalena Medio. When Uribe Sierra was murdered at his ranch in 1983, young Álvaro flew there in

Escobar's helicopter. President Betancur and important members of the regional elite attended Uribe Sierra's funeral, demonstrating their willingness to overlook dubious business ventures from which they benefited.

One of President Uribe's ranches in Córdoba bordered one that belonged to Salvatore Mancuso, the paramilitary "entrepreneur of coercion," who had served as a Convivir commander in Córdoba, and became one of the leading figures of the AUC. Uribe affected to know him only as a fellow cattle rancher – just as he knew the Ochoas only as horse traders.[240] As governor of Antioquia, Uribe's "Montesinos," to borrow a term from Molano, was Secretary of Government Pedro Juan Moreno Villa. He was alleged, by a former US DEA chief, to be the country's leading importer of potassium permanganate, the main chemical precursor in the manufacture of cocaine, between 1994 and 1998 – a period that overlapped with Uribe's term.[241] Juan Moreno was one of Uribe's campaign advisors in 2002. General del Río, the "pacifier" of Urabá, was dismissed by Pastrana for links to the paramilitaries, and celebrated an act of protest (*acto de desagravio*) in response. The event, organized in May 1999 by Juan Moreno and General Bedoya's political movement, Fuerza Colombia, served as a launching pad for Uribe's presidential campaign. Like Moreno, General del Río was a campaign advisor.[242]

Based on his choice of friends, neighbors, advisors, and ministers, Antonio Caballero, arguably Colombia's leading humorist – following the political murder in 1999 of the person who had previously held that distinction – noted that Uribe appeared fond of bad company.[243] Whatever the nature of his relationship to narco-paramilitarism in Córdoba and Antioquia, the indignation with which the Clinton administration and the US media treated Samper, contaminated by mere receipt of campaign finance from the drug lords, seems comical in retrospect.

Although he extradited more traffickers than any president in Colombian history, Uribe's links to the inmost nexus of narcotics, and its peculiar forms of terrorism, would appear to be far more intimate than Samper's; not one extradited trafficker was a ranking paramilitary. Initially, however, Uribe was warmly embraced by the US government, as well as the Colombian oligarchy and middle class. *Semana* declared him "Man of the Year" in 2002. This was because, in the eyes of the majority of Colombians and US policy-makers, he did not represent narcotics, paramilitarism, or clientelist politics as usual. His public image was that of a true believer in counterinsurgency as a means of extending state power.

As at previous conjunctures, in the late 1990s the reform-minded fraction of the ruling class did not represent the ruling class as a whole, much less the nation. In their war against the state and its paramilitary allies, insurgencies stepped up campaigns of kidnapping, extortion, bombings, and even massacres, which brought the war closer to the everyday lives of city and town dwellers of all classes, races, genders, and generations. Fanned by media hysteria, these tactics helped lead a majority of voters to opt, in a quixotic quest for "security," for right-wing authoritarianism in line with cold war principles of counterinsurgency.

9

The Edge of the Precipice, 2002–5

President Uribe has made Colombian society one that is professing
the culture of paramilitarism . . . In Colombia, we are headed
toward a mafia state.

Ramiro Bejarano, former head of DAS (2006)

Plan Colombia failed in terms of drug eradication, but succeeded in
modernizing the Colombian Armed Forces, which lacked hardware,
especially helicopters, and specially trained fighting units; paramilitaries
consolidated political, social, and territorial influence in territories
formerly held by the insurgencies. By targeting FARC areas almost
exclusively, Plan Colombia helped paramilitaries vertically integrate their
criminal enterprise and turn it into a political instrument.[244] Debate on
the Justice and Peace Law, regulating paramilitary participation in official
politics and civil society, was structured around the opposition of
memory and justice versus peace and forgetting. It was an odd way
to frame the fate of a group that had admittedly relied on massacres, drug
trafficking, and expropriation in its push to eradicate the insurgencies.[245]

The need to forget and pardon without truth or justice was related to
the AUC's drive to enter formal politics, of course, but also to systematic
ties to the Colombian police and armed forces documented in reports by
Human Rights Watch, Amnesty International, and the US State Department.[246] The ELN, pushed to breaking point, had begun preliminary talks on negotiations with Uribe's government. The FARC has
been excluded and – facing 18,000 mobilized troops – subject to the
largest US-backed military offensive in history, under Plan Patriota,
while those fighting alongside or in lieu of the state were politically
incorporated.

I   A New Feudalism

In 2003–5, the armed Right's electoral power endangered the bipartisan monopoly for the first time since 1848. In seeking re-election and creating a legal architecture for legitimate paramilitary participation in state and society – now fused under the concept of the "communitarian state" – Uribe split his party, strengthening the central government by linking it to dispersed regional power centers. The election of Uribe marked the end of the historical cycle initiated in 1982, since Uribe did not plan to negotiate with guerrillas without first inflicting decisive military defeat. No president since Laureano Gómez had identified so closely with opinions that held sway among the military high command, regional elites, and their allies in government. The reactionary coalition, born during Betancur's peace process, hardened against Barco's municipal reforms and Gaviria's departmental reforms, and, through paramilitarism, landed elites and regional-local governments blocked both central government reforms and peace initiatives. Now they had an ally in the Casa de Nariño.

After Uribe's assumption of the presidency, the paramilitaries tightened their grip over patronage and politics.[247] At the top, there were numerous commanders who became paramilitaries to bury the record of what they had done as traffickers. These men were known mainly for their reputations in the mafia underworld: Francisco Javier Zuluaga, José Vicente Castaño (Carlos and Fidel's brother), Hernán and Jesús Giraldo, Rodrigo Tovar Puro, a.k.a. "Jorge 40," Diego Fernando Murillo, a.k.a. "Don Berna."[248] Once negotiations began, all except Castaño appeared in uniform as *comandantes paramilitares.* They were given a nickname that played on their opportunism – "the parachutists" (*los paracaidistas*) – and were said to be trying to get their *paraportes* (a play on the word *pasaporte*) to avoid extradition to the USA.[249]

Córdoba – the bastion of the Castaño brothers and Salvatore Mancuso – was the birthplace of "Colombia Viva," a political movement designed to rally support for the incorporation of the AUC into state institutions. Santa Fe de Ralito, located in the southern part of the department, was chosen by the AUC as the place to negotiate with government. Colombia Viva elected two congresspersons from Córdoba in 2002. The AUC exercised oversight of the University of Córdoba, managing the only hospital in the southern part of the department. In their municipalities of

Tierralta and Valencia, considered the political capitals of the AUC, both mayors elected in 2003 were from Colombia Viva. Other candidates withdrew, citing paramilitary threats. Along with two others, on 10 April 2005, Departmental Congressman Orlando Benítez Palencia was assassinated by paramilitaries from Don Berna's Héroes of Tolová Bloc in Valencia. Benítez failed to heed warnings not to run for mayor there.[250]

For Enrique Santos Calderón, editor of *El Tiempo*, narcotraffickers, paramilitaries, and political bosses (*gamonales*) had fused along the Atlantic coast.[251] The department of Magdalena, controlled by Hernán Giraldo and Rodrigo Tovar, provided one of the best examples. The AUC's candidate for governor, Trino Luna Correa, won in 2003 after running unopposed. Other candidates resigned, citing paramilitary threats and harassment, and more voters cast blank ballots than voted for Luna. The AUC secured victory for three senators as well as three representatives. When Efraín Escalante insisted on running for mayor of Concordia, in spite of AUC threats, he was assassinated. In Magdalena's capital city, Santa Marta, paramilitaries quickly amassed a fortune by charging taxes on the trucks bringing goods to container ships that dock in the port's deep harbor. Everyone from street vendors to store owners paid them taxes.[252] Through Dibulla, Mingueo, and Palomino, towns located at the foot of the Sierra Nevada de Santa Marta across the departmental border in La Guajira, they moved drugs and guns unmolested, despite considerable army and police presence on the roads.

In Magdalena and La Guajira, paramilitaries working for Giraldo and "Jorge 40" controlled intelligence, gambling, prostitution, private security, protection rackets, contraband, money laundering, and most of the cocaine business. In Cesar, the cattle-ranching department where "Jorge 40" had once served as finance secretary, the picture was similar. As in Magdalena, the governor ran unopposed in 2003, after other candidates resigned in the face of AUC threats. As in Magdalena, he won, although the number of blank votes outnumbered votes for him. In La Guajira, which borders Venezuela – and, along with Cesar and Magdalena, forms part of the north coast region defined by the Sierra Nevada de Santa Marta – the mayor and ten city council members were arrested in Riohacha, the capital, in September 2004. They had allegedly funneled health care block grants to paramilitaries run by "Jorge 40" and Jesús Giraldo (Hernán's brother, also wanted for extradition to the USA on trafficking charges).[253]

Antioquia provided another example of flagrant paramilitary control, and while a minority questioned it in private, few dared to do so in public.[254] Despite the ostensible demobilization of the Bloque Cacique Nutibara (BCN) in November 2003, Diego Fernando Murillo, a.k.a. "Don Berna" in the underworld, a.k.a. "Adolfo Paz" in the AUC, continued to rule over the city to a degree Escobar had only dreamed of. Born in Túlua, Valle, the center of *pájaro* operations in the 1950s, after leaving the EPL, Murillo was a *sicario* who worked his way to the top of Escobar's organization. He survived various rounds of internecine warfare to become the undisputed mafia boss of Medellín.[255] By 2005, he commanded Bloques Héroes de Granada, Calima, Libertadores del Sur, Pacífico, and Héroes de Tolová from his seat at the negotiating table in Santa Fe de Ralito, until he "gave himself up" in late May 2005. He agreed to be held under government supervision on a ranch in Córdoba, near the seat of negotiations, in exchange for political benefits under the pending Justice and Peace Law. He was later taken to a maximum security prison in response to US government pressure after assassinating the departmental congressmen from Córdoba, but was then returned to a local prison just south of Medellín, in his own territory, where he carried on with business as usual.

In 2004, while his private army worked to take over cable television services, Don Berna's candidates won 30 posts as heads of local neighborhood advisory boards (*Juntas de Acción Comunal*) in Medellín, and dominated construction, real estate, finance, transport, wholesale, and retail. Through the infamous "Envigado Office," Don Berna supervised extortion, intelligence gathering, surveillance, contract killing, recruitment and training of assassins, auto theft, bank robbery, gambling and prostitution, drug sales, money laundering, and private security. Through his NGO, "Corporación Democracia," Don Berna had begun to select candidates for the legislative elections of March 2006.[256]

Even in Bogotá, similar processes were under way. Paramilitaries controlled the main wholesale food market, as well as the duty-free markets (*sanandresitos*), profiting from local peasant production, networks of unofficial informants, pirated CDs, and cell phone calls. Paramilitaries were estimated to make 400 million pesos (more than $160,000) per month from extortion in the *sanandresitos* alone. They also controlled many of the capital's prostitution rings, and engaged in widespread kidnapping and contract killing – the very tactics against which they were supposed to be fighting – in order to expand their holdings. They were involved in white slavery, and invested in stores, car dealerships, gas stations, construction, gambling, contraband, and motels. According to an official report, they dominated entire slum districts, like Ciudad Bolívar in the south, using gangs to take over local economies. One of the authors of said report warned that Bogotá was becoming similar to Don Berna's Medellín.[257]

In Bucaramanga, Santander, a delegate who participated in a comparative research project on paramilitarism spoke of the "Don Bernization" of the city, whereby poor youth from the northern slum districts – Comunas 1 and 2 (fifty-three neighborhoods) – were being recruited to work in illegal economies dominated by the paramilitary mafia. Bucaramanga Metropolitan Area (AMB) was shared out between Ivan Duque, "Ernesto Báez," leader of the Central Bolívar Bloc (BCB), and "Jorge 40," chief of the Northern Bloc (NB). Stores of all types in La Cumbe and Bucarica in Comunas 1 and 2 paid 6,000 pesos per day ($2.50) in taxes, while mechanics and shoemakers in Comuna 3 paid the same. Car washes charged bus drivers 2,000 pesos per day – 8,000 if the driver wanted security against stick-ups. Taxi drivers paid 3,000 pesos, and street vendors 500 pesos, for the use of public space. Curfew went into effect after 9 P.M., and young women were prohibited from wearing miniskirts, or revealing cleavage. Drug users, criminals, adulterous women, and prostitutes were "cleansed." Yet, like paramilitaries nationwide, in Bucaramanga they recruited young women and men into lucrative drug and prostitution rings.[258]

Over time, the paramilitary drug mafia organized unemployed youth into a disciplined, mobile counterinsurgent army of labor. This was far beyond anything Marx imagined when he described the role of the lumpenproletariat in mid-nineteenth-century France. Unemployed slum dwellers, especially from Antioquia, the coffee axis, and the Santanders, had colonized much of the Atlantic coast. The colonization of the coffee frontier in the nineteenth century led to the foundation of new municipalities under Liberal or Conservative party patronage; while the second wave of colonization, from slums or small towns in the interior to other small towns or slums, mainly those of the national periphery, favored the AUC. While the FARC had abandoned "the combination of all forms of struggle," their opponents employed it more effectively than ever.[259] They scored their first key victory in the congressional elections of March 2002, in which they won between 30 and 35 per cent of seats.

A new generation of soldiers had replaced the battle-hardened veterans created in the mold of the Castaños and Mancuso, however. They did not wear uniforms or live in remote mountainous or lowland regions, but moved anonymously in cities and towns, performing the daily tasks of administration, occupation, and accumulation. They were more like the *pájaros* than Castaño's troops. At the bottom, many of the new recruits were unarmed, and, unlike the Convivirs, did not sport telltale two-way radios on the hip. In Valledupar, Santa Marta, Cartagena, the cities of the north coast; Bucaramanga and Barrancabermeja in the Santanders; Villavicencio and Puerto Asis in the southern jungles; Medellín, Cali, and Bogotá in the Andean heartlands; Pereira and Manizales in the coffee axis, they could be seen selling cell phone calls, operating fruit stands, selling CDs and sunglasses, driving taxis, running auto repair shops, guarding public buildings and private businesses, "collecting bills" (*cobrando facturas*), monitoring movements in and out of neighborhoods, protecting politicians and businessmen, riding around on motorcycles running "errands," or sitting in restaurants, bars, bakeries, and cafes, eavesdropping on people's conversations.

II "Judicial Bulletproofing"

In late June 2005, the Colombian Congress – 35 per cent of it controlled by paramilitaries, according to Mancuso and José Vicente Castaño – approved the Justice and Peace Law, and in late July Uribe signed it, in spite of domestic and international controversy. The director of Human Rights Watch-Americas Watch warned that the law would "launder the criminal records of top paramilitary commanders – including some of the country's most powerful drug lords – while allowing them to keep their wealth and maintain their control over much of the country."[260] A senior "violentologist" predicted a scenario of Italianization that would "produce an order based on crime and cruelty" in which "terror and the superconcentration of wealth" would be distinguishing features.[261]

Just as the discourse of "anti-terrorism" denied guerrilla insurgencies the possibility of achieving political recognition as anti-state actors, under article 72 of the Justice and Peace Law, the AUC secured political status as "subversives" and "rebels."[262] This would allow top commanders to avoid lengthy prison terms and/or extradition. Sentences would carry a maximum of six and a half years. A team of twenty prosecutors would be given a maximum of sixty days to investigate crimes. There would be no unraveling of command structures, logistics, transport routes, finances, investments, political alliances, or other aspects of paramilitarism that would reveal kinship with official power.

Former Uribe supporter, Senator Rafael Pardo – who, as minister of defense under Gaviria, came up with the idea of Convivirs – helped author a bill that would have required investigation into the financial, military, and political structures of paramilitary organizations, along with some form of reparations for the victims of paramilitary crimes against humanity. He contended that the "Justice and Peace" legislation made "a farce of justice," and warned that it could "lead to the legal establishment of a political model based on organized crime."[263] Former president Gaviria, aiming to save the Liberal Party from collapsing under the pressure of *uribismo*, echoed Pardo. "Mafias have taken over various departments," he insisted, "not only in terms of drugs, but in terms of administration . . . One sees the president very comfortable with these situations."[264] The two agreed that Uribe's Justice and Peace Law would grant impunity to the leaders of organized crime, facilitating mafia penetration of the state in the regions, cities, and *municipios*.

Since the Bush administration would not finance but a fraction of the improvised, legally dubious demobilization process – the costs of which Ambassador Wood estimated at $170 million – Uribe initially looked to Europe and the rest of the world. US Ambassador William Wood declared Mancuso's appearance before the Colombian Congress in July 2004 "absurd," and insisted that paramilitaries were not political actors, but rather "criminals, drug traffickers, murderers, and thieves." Yet in 2006, the US government set aside $20 million for their ostensible disarmament.[265]

Reflecting the relative power of human rights organizations in the EU as compared to the USA, when they met in Cartagena in February 2005, European governments and multinational lending agencies required that paramilitary crimes against humanity be punished. Disbursement of funds hinged on the passage of legislation that mandated investigation, incarceration, and some form of reparations. Following the UN, the EU roundly rejected Uribe's Justice and Peace Law as unacceptable according to international standards.[266] Support for "democratic security" policies and peace with the paramilitaries (however qualified) was nevertheless a startling retreat from the support for a negotiated peace with the FARC and the ELN – the lynchpin of EU diplomacy from the 1980s through the early Pastrana years.

In a show of how far EU foreign policy had shifted right after acceding to the Anglo-American occupation of Iraq, in April 2005 German Defense Minister Hans Georg Wagner expressed enthusiasm for "democratic security."[267] The contrast between the treatment afforded the AUC versus the FARC was remarkable. The FARC had never agreed to a cease-fire under Pastrana, so they did not discredit themselves by violating it, as the AUC did on a daily basis. FARC territory was slated for takeover in the form of the Plan Patriota.

Plan Patriota helped turn the Colombian conflict into a source of ongoing regional diplomatic tension. Though this $700 million plan was chiefly funded by the Colombian government, it was supervised by 800 US advisors and 600 mercenaries, and relied on the USA for logistics and military intelligence support, as well as over $100 million in "aid" per year. Initiated in late 2003, to drive the FARC out of a 116-mile heartland of Caquetá, Meta, Guaviare, and Vaupés, and extradite FARC leaders to the USA, Plan Patriota was Operación Marquetalia writ large (plus extradition), and spread the war to Venezuela and Ecuador. Some 20,000 Ecuadorian troops massed along the Colombian border in April 2006, while in Venezuela, more than 100 Colombians served prison time for plotting to kill Hugo Chávez in coordination with Colombian paramilitaries and DAS – the intelligence service answerable only to President Uribe.

Paramilitaries were permitted to hold on to the country's best lands – close to half of *all* cultivable land, according to the Comptroller General's Office – along with the most profitable networks of narcotics production, transport, and distribution, not to mention legal front businesses. The "demobilization" process began in November 2003, accelerated in late 2004, and left more than 30,000 former paramilitaries demobilized by March 2005.[268] Commanders declared that rather than go to jail for "excesses" committed in "defense of the fatherland," they would take up arms again. Extradition to the USA was out of the question; ditto reparations for the families of victims. In April 2005, with negotiations on the verge of unraveling, the political spokesman of the AUC, Ivan Duque, a.k.a. "Ernesto Báez," threatened to "return to the mountains," but once Uribe signed the Justice and Peace Law, Báez called for the formation of a political movement, and described the parastate formation process with candor: "We have penetrated, in a permanent way, the political process, building local and regional power structures . . . Our goal is to outlive the war and transform ourselves into a democratic movement that will offer voters an alternative."[269]

Salvatore Mancuso announced intentions to make a career in politics, and praised Uribe's law since for recognizing the AUC as "political actors" – an objective first stated at the proto-national paramilitary conference in 1994.[270] Mancuso contended that since the absence of the state in guerrilla zones had obligated paramilitaries to take up arms in "self-defense," the AUC's troops were victims, and therefore as deserving of reparations as victims of paramilitary atrocities.[271] José Vicente Castaño echoed him, emphasizing the AUC's family ties to official Colombian politics, demanding that paramilitaries be given "judicial bulletproofing" against extradition and prison terms. He predicted the AUC would improve its already strong position in Congress in legislative elections in March 2006; his prediction came true, as citizens in twenty-two of Colombia's thirty-two departments voted further right than they had in 2002.[272] Discussing plans to run for office once "judicial obstacles" were cleared, Mancuso suggested that many former AUC commanders would follow his lead.[273]

The results of the legislative elections of March 2006 suggested that, wary of extradition, paramilitaries took their cues from the US government. On the one hand, extradition warrants were issued for fifty FARC commanders in a federal grand jury indictment in the District of Columbia, with US Attorney General Alberto Gonzales stating, in the face of all evidence to the contrary, that the FARC was responsible for most of Colombia's cocaine production. He added that the indictment "strikes at the very heart of the FARC narcotics operation that has flooded our communities with cocaine."[274] The expulsion of a handful of openly paramilitary candidates from the most prominent of pro-Uribe parties, on the other hand, led to greater paramilitary support for traditional machine politicians. This camouflaged, but did not diminish, paramilitary dominance of politics in the regions. Jorge 40, lord of the north coast, waited until political alignments were in place, demobilizing just before the elections in March 2006. Maintaining a low political profile, Jorge 40 obtained the most favorable electoral results of any paramilitary chieftain.[275]

III Scorched Earth in the Cattle Republic

Paramilitaries were estimated to have expropriated some 5 million hectares between 1997 and 2003 – the largest land grab in Colombian history. One Colombian analyst asserted that the power of the landed fraction of its ruling class made Colombia uniquely atavistic, while another dubbed the country a "cattle republic."[276] The agrarian counter-reform carried out by "self-defense" forces, as paramilitaries called themselves, favored palm and banana plantations, as well as logging companies and cattle ranchers.[277] The numbers are telling: in 1987, 35 million hectares were devoted to cattle ranching, and in 2001, 41.7 million. In 1984, ranches larger than 500 hectares occupied 32.7 per cent of the land; in 1996, 44.6 per cent; in 2001, 61.2 per cent. By 2004, 0.4 per cent of landowners possessed 61 per cent of all titled land, while rural poverty was up from 82.6 per cent in 2001 to 85 per cent in 2003.

Of course, figures cannot tell the stories of the displaced, most of whom, in addition to trauma, experience discrimination and political persecution in new locations.[278] Barring a major political reversal, of course, it was unlikely that more than a handful of the displaced would return home, and less likely that their land (mostly untitled) would be returned to them. Only one in three received government assistance of any kind. And though much has been made of the 15 million hectares of tropical rain forest destroyed and planted with coca, somewhere between 75 and 100 million hectares of jungle had been cleared to make way for cattle. The Comptroller General's Office spoke of "seigneurial power of an anti-democratic stripe" in the countryside, naming narco-paramilitaries as wielders of "real power" in the regions and municipalities.[279]

Along with increasing land concentration, expropriation, and dispossession, aerial fumigation under Plan Colombia has been an enormously costly and destructive endeavor, causing widespread respiratory and skin infections in the civilian population, especially children and the elderly, killing licit as well as illicit crops, and poisoning rivers and soils.[280] Nevertheless, from 2002 to 2004, Washington and Bogotá claimed unprecedented success in their campaign against coca; in December

2002, a UN study alleged that planting had been cut by 30 per cent, to 252,000 acres.[281]

During 2003, over 35,000 acres were destroyed every month – according to legislation approved by the US Congress in early December 2003, even forests in National Parks, which contain 70 per cent of Colombia's water and 10 million hectares of officially protected forest, became fair game. In 2005, fumigation and/or manual eradication were undertaken in Parque Tayrona in Magdalena, La Macarena in Caquetá, and Catatumbo in Northern Santander, in which less than 1 per cent of surface area was dedicated to coca cultivation.[282]

In the far south, in Putumayo, "Towns dedicated to the harvest and production of cocaine have been abandoned like ghost towns in the old American West, their stores empty, their people vanished."[283] Using highly concentrated doses of Monsanto's Round-Up Ultra mixed with Cosmo-Flux, a chemical compound formerly supplied by ICI that made glyphosate stick to whatever it touched, such fumigation was an integral part of Plan Colombia after 2000. Spraying this toxic compound, Colombian pilots and US mercenaries destroyed fish, wildlife, livestock, rivers, and legal crops, as well as coca fields throughout southern Colombia.[284] In many cases, coca settlers have simply replanted further out on the frontier.

Chemical warfare needs to be viewed a part of the broader counter-insurgent strategy. "Fumigation is a mode . . . whose hidden objective is to get settlers and peasants out of their regions to prevent them from helping . . . the subversion . . . It serves the same function as para-military terror: to drain the water from the sea."[285] Even as fumigation reached record levels, with nearly 136,000 hectares sprayed, 114,000 hectares remained in 2004. There was no "improvement," as net coca production remained close to 1999 levels – as opposed to 50 per cent less, according to the stated goals of Plan Colombia's authors. Prices of cocaine and heroin on US streets continued to decrease slightly, while for every 32 hectares of coca fumigated, one was eradicated. Including the number of hectares fumigated, coca production in Colombia was greater in 2005 than in 2003, and remained just below the record set in 2002. By 2006, it was clear that whether or not the reductions in 2002–3 were a mirage, coca cultivation had hit record levels again, as farmers replanted, relocated, or both. Aerial fumigation of over 2,500 square miles of Colombian territory, much of it jungle and rain forest, at a narrow economic cost of at least $160,000 per square mile, succeeded only in reducing coca production locally, often temporarily.

Of course, in the absence of any crop-substitution program, insurgent and counterinsurgent terror on the coca frontiers can only increase, as even the RAND Corporation studies recognized. It has also created diplomatic problems with neighboring governments in Quito and Caracas, which contended that plans Colombia and Patriota had led to increasing violations of their sovereignty. But this was not a cost to make the Bush-Uribe regime blink.

10

War as Peace, 2005–6

During the last five years, the Colombian people have produced the single greatest success story in Latin America.
R. Nicholas Burns, US Undersecretary of State for Political Affairs (2006)

I Unifying Theory and Practice

The executive branch in Washington hailed Uribe's "democratic security" policies, which focused on integrating civilians into the repressive branches of the state in order to defeat insurgencies and extend central government authority, as a model for counterinsurgency. While they have not succeeded against entrenched guerrilla insurgencies, democratic security politics have allowed paramilitary forces to extend their control of political, economic, and social life to new regions. They have also reinforced internal colonialism and violated Geneva Protocols regulating relations between civilians and combatants.

Any interpretation of the armed conflict carries specific legal, political, and military ramifications.[286] Using arguments put forth in a book written by an advisor, in late January 2005, President Uribe announced to his diplomatic corps that neither war nor armed conflict existed in Colombia.[287] That, of course, would imply politically recognized warring parties. Instead, an embattled state and civil society was fighting (and, with the help of an "international community" led by the USA, would soon defeat) "terrorism." Public debate in Colombia frequently hinges on semantics, and the political significance of language is not lost on anyone.[288] If the problem could be redefined as "terrorism," it would mean the end of pressure for a negotiated – that is, political – solution to armed conflict with the FARC.

In the age of Guantánamo and Abu Ghraib, acceptance of new nomenclature would also have allowed Uribe to ignore Protocol II of the Geneva Conventions, which obliges governments as well as insurgents to distinguish between civilians and combatants. Meanwhile, Uribe advanced in preliminary talks on peace negotiations with the ELN in Havana, in keeping with the model of fragmented peace first established under Gaviria. After 11 September 2001, before becoming US Attorney General, as White House Special Counsel, Alberto Gonzales called Protocol IV of the Geneva Conventions "quaint" and "archaic," while in June 2005, President Bush called an Amnesty International report on torture and human rights abuse in Guantánamo "absurd." Uribe may have been hoping to capitalize on new imperial doctrines regarding anti-terrorism, human rights, and international law.[289]

Though largely beyond the scope of this book, the relationship between cold war anti-communism and post-cold war anti-terrorism is worthy of brief consideration. As cold war counterinsurgents under Ronald Reagan, leaders of President George W. Bush's "global war on terrorism" fought old battles under new rubrics. Colonial wars in Iraq and Afghanistan were similar to those in Vietnam, Guatemala, and El Salvador, insofar as planners and commanders targeted civilians as a way to fight armed insurgencies. The counterinsurgent core of cold war anti-communism was retained in the "global war on terrorism," making Uribe and the Colombian generals contemporary rather than anachronistic.[290]

II "The Changing Same:" Urabá

Counterinsurgent theory holds that in guerrilla warfare, the distinction between civilians and combatants breaks down. In practice, the Colombian military had no regard for human rights or the Geneva Conventions, for they did not face civilian courts until 1991. They viewed civilian oversight as an obstacle to waging the counterinsurgent war against Colombian people, and Uribe's positions were in line with the military's. Well after the disintegration of the Soviet Union and Eastern bloc, Uribe, like the Colombian high command, retained a political philosophy rooted in the cold war, but recycled under the rubric of "anti-terrorism."

A prominent sociologist noted that the generals' "hypothesis of war" was "impervious to change."[291] As if to illustrate the consequences of this approach, on 21–22 February 2005, near the Peace Community of San José de Apartadó, four community members – including Luis Eduardo Guerra, one of the community's leaders and founders – three children, aged two, six, and eleven, and one adolescent, aged seventeen, were murdered. Some were slaughtered with machetes and their bodies dismembered.[292] According to local residents, who refused to testify before state authorities for fear of reprisal, army soldiers were responsible. The army provided confusing, contradictory statements about its actions during the massacre.

Leaders like Luis Eduardo Guerra had traveled to the USA and Europe to explain their situation and efforts to ameliorate it. As a result of international pressure, an OAS Inter-American Human Rights Court decision mandated that members of San José receive security guarantees from the Colombian government. The February massacre, however, brought the total number of community members assassinated to 152 (19 of them at the hands of the FARC), which demonstrated the limits of international solidarity.[293] As practitioners of militant, non-violent neutrality, with strong ties to international human rights organizations, however, residents of San José continued to insist that in order to live and produce in peace, they needed all armed forces, including government troops and police, out of their community.

They threatened to pick up and move if the government insisted on setting up a police station in the town, which would have made them a target for FARC incursions. But former minister of defense, Jorge Alberto Uribe, said there could be no peace without the protection of the police and armed forces. President Uribe went further: "There are good people in the community, but some of its leaders, patrons, and defenders have been signaled by people who live there as FARC auxiliaries."[294] Given leftist insurgencies, all forms of social protest and mobilization were suspect, even criminal, because insurgents were thought to direct them in secret.

This led to the conclusion that if civilian supporters of guerrillas were not first identified and then either co-opted or targeted, the state and its US-trained and -funded troops could not win their war. By early April 2005, a police station had been installed in San José, and most of its remaining 400 inhabitants had left to found a new municipality, La Holandita, without a school, medical services, electricity, running water, or sewerage. There was a single bathroom for the entire community. In May, only five families remained in the original settlement, but police were there in larger numbers.[295]

In line with an economic development model driven by export agribusiness and financed by foreign capital, former community lands in San José were likely to be targeted for African palm plantation development. Since palm plantations required deforestation and heavy irrigation, they represented a danger to rivers and forests, as well as the community.[296] In his first public interview, José Vicente Castaño took personal credit for the rise of the African palm and agribusiness in Urabá. Castaño had invested, convinced others to invest, and gone in search of new regions for investment.

Known as the AUC's behind-the-scenes strategist, Castaño, a.k.a. "the Professor," offered a rudimentary theory of state formation. The AUC secured regions for investment, and the Colombian state followed investors: "We've got to take rich people to invest in regions all over the country, and that's one of our missions as *comandantes*."[297] Thus the African palm – to be implanted, like state sovereignty, via terror and expropriation – represented a threat to the survival of Afro-Colombians and mestizos in San José, as well as indigenous reserves along the lower Atrato, Cacarica, Curvaradó, Jiguamiandó, and Salaqi rivers.[298] "The extermination to which we have been subject by the armed forces, which have nakedly acted with paramilitarism," the Peace Community of San José observed, "is not our invention nor is it a question of statistics. Our victims have faces, histories, and families."[299]

III   "Return to the Source:" Cauca

Cauca's indigenous groups are currently at the forefront of radical-popular movements in Colombia. They led the largest mass march in Cauca's history (60,000) in September 2004, against "democratic security" policies and the proposed free trade agreement with the USA.[300] In March 2005, they organized a referendum on free trade in which 70 per cent of the population participated, with 98 per cent voting against free trade with the USA, in a process international observers considered transparent. A former mayor of Caldono, Vicente Otero, was one of the key organizers of the campaign, and on 21 May, DAS agents searched his house and arrested twenty townsmen and women. Warrants were issued for another 200.[301] Caldono, located in the same area as the war zone of Toribío, Jambaló, and Tocueyó, was then destroyed by FARC cylinder bombs on 3–5 July.

Northern Cauca, where insurgencies had been encrusted for over twenty years, became a strategic rearguard because Plan Patriota targeted the other side of the cordillera in Caquetá and Meta. Colombian generals argued that the *macizo* region – where the eastern and central cordilleras part ways – had become a second "Caguán," a reference to the site of negotiations between the FARC and Pastrana in Caquetá. Caldono's school was therefore turned into a barracks, while its sports field became a heliport. According to the mayor's office, 2,400 were displaced, over half of them women and children.[302]

When visiting Bogotá in April 2005, US Secretary of State Condoleezza Rice may not have been aware of the importance of her unwavering support for the counterinsurgent cause. As she arrived, the FARC had overrun the Nasa town of Tacueyó.[303] The armed forces took Toribío only after nine days of sustained combat with the FARC that began on April 14 and spread along a fourteen-mile stretch of the northern Andes.[304] Rice uncritically repeated Uribe's specious claim to have achieved control over all of Colombia's municipalities – ignorant, apparently, of events in northern Cauca and the shake-up within the high command. Talk of a "definitive solution" to Colombia's armed conflict was uninformed at best, ominous at worst. Following Rice's lead, Uribe promised to undertake "definitive action" to "defeat terrorists" in northern Cauca.[305]

Though Rice declared, "Concrete improvements in security and rule of law are fostering a culture of lawfulness in Colombia and a sense of security for its citizens," headlines flatly contradicted her. The only party implementing the rule of law was caught in the crossfire between the FARC and the military. The military high command, four of whose members were forced to resign after disagreeing about the effectiveness of joint task force operations, had been caught flat-footed. This was by far the most convincing demonstration to date that the FARC was as militarily capable in 2005 as it was in 1995, and that democratic security had not been effective in defeating the insurgencies.[306]

The attacks on Toribío, like the attacks on San José, struck at the heart of the radical-popular movement in Colombia. Where the FARC could not be blamed for San José, Toribío was yet another illustration of their colonial *criollo* attitudes toward indigenous people in Cauca and else-where.[307] The death of a nine-year-old boy and the destruction wrought by gas cylinder bombs were shown around the world. Nasa men and women mobilized their "indigenous guards," which totaled some 7,000, and, armed with wooden canes connoting leadership status, hiked to the FARC's mountaintop position to tell them not to launch bombs on the town.

Here were democratic security policies, based on non-liberal com-munity traditions of non-violent conflict resolution, that promoted the rule of law, government protection of constitutional rights, democratic political participation, and popular sovereignty. As he had after the massacre in San José, however, Uribe insinuated links between the communities and the FARC. By late May 2005, there were arrest warrants for 200 Nasa, accused of guerrilla ties.[308] As they had with the FARC (and, previously, the AUC), community leaders reiterated to President Uribe and the military the need to rid their territories of all parties in the war system.

Discussing military-police presence and dismissing alleged links to the insurgency in one of Uribe's "communitarian councils," a group led by Nasa Congressman Daniel Piñacué walked out in protest against the president's incomprehension of Nasa modes of conflict resolution. The Colombian National Indigenous Organization (ONIC) labeled the "communitarian council" a "media spectacle," explaining that the representatives of "distinct instances of the government, orchestrated by the president, dialogue among themselves, impose their position, their biased reports, their policies and interests, and impede questioning or criticism."[309] Clearly, Uribe and indigenous people had incompatible visions of authority, democracy, security, and popular sovereignty.

As in San José, the police arrived in Toribío to stay.[310] The state would not permit neutrality of citizens in the war it had promised to win, and demanded collaboration against the FARC. Those who went along would be rewarded, while those who did not would be suspect. Com-munity leader Ezekiel Vitonás, who traveled to New York City to address the UN in May 2005, criticized Uribe: "Identity, unity, territory, and culture are the four pillars contemplated in the constitution, but self-determination of indigenous peoples is not upheld." Vitonás specified that "self-determination" meant developing a way of life and subsistence, based on tradition, and defending it in the face of threats.[311]

Indigenous rights and self-determination did merit mention in the US Senate foreign aid bill for 2006, but were not high on President Bush's list of priorities in Colombia. Echoing the justification for US foreign policy in El Salvador in the early 1980s, Secretary Rice repeated that, while much improvement remained to be done on human rights, coca eradication, and so forth, Colombia was "on the road." This fit with the Bush administration's vision of Iraq, fashioned in part by veterans from counterinsurgent campaigns in Central America, for whom El Salvador was used as an example of imperial success. In January 2006, Secretary Rice and President Bush mentioned Colombia as a template for counter-insurgent democracy. Each spoke independently of the need for the putative Iraqi government to "clear" Iraqi territories of insurgencies and "hold" them against insurgent threat. This was the language used to explain the goals of Plan Patriota. On the MacNeal/Lehrer *NewsHour* in December 2005, President Bush used Colombia as an example of imperial success on what he called the "heart and soul" front, and employed the language of "clear and hold" in his "National Strategy for Victory in Iraq" in January 2006.[312] Apparently, nothing succeeds quite like success.

Conclusion: Amnesia by Decree³¹³

We just want to forget the past.
> Manuel Mariano, demobilized paramilitary (2006)

Until the end of the nineteenth century, frequent but small-scale civil wars made Colombia representative within Latin America, but since *la Violencia* of the 1940s and 1950s – a conflict that left at least 200,000 people dead – its historical course has been more violent than those of its neighbors. In spite of diverse trajectories, social democratic electoral politics, supported by radical-popular organizations, characterize the current scene in South America. In Colombia, in contrast, militarily strong Left insurgencies, imperially supported police and armed forces, and a semi-autonomous, increasingly powerful coalition of private right-wing narco-armies weakened the radical-popular movement. Patterns of counterinsurgent terror against civilians established in *la Violencia* were reinforced during the cold war, and repackaged under the anti-terrorist rubric after 11 September 2001. Not for the first time, in response to struggles for peace and justice, terror and official amnesia have become the lingua franca of Colombian politics and society.

The first historic defeat for radical-popular forces came in 1879. Although the contest in Cauca was regional, Liberal "Independents" backed Rafael Núñez's bid for dominance, so its political implications were national. In the "Age of Capital" (1848–76), official Colombian politics had been marked by continuous popular mobilization, as subordinate groups defined new ideas of citizenship and popular sover-eignty in discourse and practice. In Cauca, ex-slaves, free persons of color, indigenous communities, and frontier settlers from Antioquia participated in a vigorous republican political culture, in which equality, fraternity, and liberty were ideas to be fought for. They struggled for a place in the new republic, challenging racial and bureaucratic domination, colonial modes of exploitation, and the spatial configuration of territory. The state was called on to help them in their efforts, and they demanded that it adjudicate local and regional conflicts with landed oligarchs. The potential for a political opening to radical-popular claims-making provoked tremendous fear in Cauca's regional elite; it helped to unite them – in spite of pronounced political differences – around an authoritarian Hispanophile Conservatism that took over the country for half a century.

Following the outbreak of the First World War, however, with coffee production continuing to surpass previous records, indigenous and peasant resistance and rebellion challenged the bipartisan monopoly of politics through direct action, local experiments in self-government, and new revolutionary socialist parties. They challenged landlord dominion through land takeovers, based on the slogan, "land belongs to the tiller." Backed by the newly formed Communist Party and trade unionists in the export enclaves (bananas, oil, gold), they pressured the Liberal administration to enact a program of social and economic reforms to redistribute land and wealth, regulate relations between organized labor and capital, and adjudicate conflict between rulers and ruled. Law 200 of 1936, designed to give land titles to occupants, was neither bourgeois, in that it did not eliminate the challenge to private property rights, nor democratic, in that it did not make landownership more widespread among the peasantry, except along the coffee axis, where a smallholding peasantry gained title to land, and access to middle-class brokers through the political parties and the coffee growers' association.

To explain Colombian uniqueness, I have emphasized how experiences of the cold war overlapped, as in a montage, with creole patterns of oligarchic rule anchored in ultramontane Catholicism, Conservative dominance, and coffee exports after the 1880s, which partially integrated subalterns into economy and society through reactionary politics. As Liberals sought to undo fifty years of Conservative rule, partisan sectarianism spread with a vengeance in the 1930s and 1940s, spawning forms of total war that targeted civilians. This stimulated, and was stimulated by, the rise of middle-class politicians, journalists, and ideologues, who aggressively staked out positions on the extreme ends of the political spectrum as a means of livelihood.

Agrarian policy in post-Second World War Colombia was similar to what Samuel Huntington would later call, in the context of the Vietnam War, "forced draft urbanization" – driving the peasantry into the cities through counterinsurgent warfare in the countryside.[314] After the 1950s, intra-elite sectarianism was finally suspended, as wounds the two parties had inflicted on one another were sutured by anti-communist counter-insurgency. Once civilian elites renounced military resolution of partisan conflict, public order became the preserve of military officials. Like the US School of the Americas, where roughly one-third more Colombian officers studied than their closest competitors from El Salvador, Korea served as a classroom for men who later occupied leading positions within the Colombian military during US imperial wars in Vietnam, Central America, and the Balkans.

Colombia's counterinsurgent terror state was built by civilian politicians who delegated repression to the military, rather than military dictators who destroyed their societies in order to save them, as happened in Central America and the Southern Cone. Permanent civil war and durable parliamentary democracy, rather than military dictatorship, made Colombia stand out, yet throughout the National Front, the use of state-of-siege legislation was the rule, not the exception. With the end of the cold war, the direct role of the military in counterinsurgency decreased as the paramilitary function increased. The trajectory of the Colombian military and civilian elites, who ran state administrations during and after the cold war, forms one side of the story of Colombia's endemic warfare and widespread political terror.

From the First World War through the mid-1940s – as US capital investment in, and government reach over, South America was extended – radical-popular mobilization challenged property rights and privileges of regionally based creole elites, undermining racial and class domination to an extent not seen since the second half of the nineteenth century. As in the 1860s, mobilization accompanied by moderate reform from above met with large-scale repression. But since the mid-twentieth century was a moment of total war in Europe and Asia, the second wave of reaction was infinitely bloodier, though hardly more technologically sophisticated, than the first. Perversely, right-wing state and parastate terror helped stimulate armed mobilization on the Left in the 1960s and 1970s, by creating migration in two directions: first, to the urban frontiers of Colombia's rapidly growing cities, and second, to the agrarian frontier, especially in the jungles of the south and the plains of the east. In those spaces, state power, even in its repressive aspect, was too weak to govern. Such areas proved to be fertile terrain for the growth of insurgencies until military-paramilitary counterinsurgency operations accelerated after 2000, under US-financed Plan Colombia.

Thanks to a shift in the productive base, toward extractive enclaves and extensive ranching and agribusiness, in the 1980s and 1990s, Left insurgencies gained in military projection, territorial reach, and local power, and lost in national political advantage, making increasing use of terror tactics that had traditionally been employed against them by opponents. There have been guerrilla insurgencies in Colombia since 1948, but their Golden Age lasted from 1978 to 1998. Colombian guerrillas grew fastest when their public image became irremediably tarnished.

With institutional support of many kinds, counterinsurgent opponents thus spread with startling velocity and increasing social acceptance between 1997 and 2005, relying on privatized, decentralized repression, and violent expropriation of territory. This fostered a wholesale reconcentration of land, wealth, and political power. During the protracted death agony of the National Front, when central governments attempted to implement reforms or negotiate peace with insurgents in 1983–84, 1987–88, 1991–92, and 1998–99, regional-local governments and *latifundistas*, old and new – joined at the hip with paramilitaries – used concentrated terror against individuals and communities perceived as subversive.

Since they were considered the "unarmed wing of the subversion," activists seeking to realize the promise – revolutionary democratic socialism – to which Salvador Allende committed his life in Chile, became targets for systematic military and paramilitary assassination campaigns after the late 1970s. A decade later, with the UP largely exterminated and Left candidates assassinated, neither the insurgencies nor the counterinsurgency considered the distinction between combatants and civilians valid. Under a neoliberal war economy in the 1990s, anarchic, atomistic individualism prevailed on urban and rural frontiers, with organized crime channeling antisocial energy into capitalist value through violence, intimidation, and physical liquidation of the electoral Left.[315]

Cocaine mafias infused fresh blood into older landed elites in the countryside, effectively putting them and the two traditional parties on life-support systems in regions and *municipios*. Multinational corporations found that narco-paramilitary "security" offered the only guarantee for private property and command of labor. Along with the collapse of prices in 1989, the paramilitary-drug mafia nexus put the last nail in the coffin of the coffee republic built in the late nineteenth century, as traffickers became the country's most powerful *latifundistas*. In the new order they have installed in regions around the country, "the land belongs to the expropriator."[316] After China, Colombia's is perhaps the largest agrarian counter-reform in the world; unlike China, though, in Colombia, counter-reform was not preceded by land reform.[317]

Modes of torture, killing, massacre, and dispossession, similar to those pioneered in *la Violencia*, were revived through new organizational vehicles in late twentieth-century Colombia. Early twenty-first-century dynamics were new, due mainly to the hurricane-like impact of the narcotics trade, paramilitary political-territorial advance, and increased US military intervention, but the presence of the past, especially *la Violencia*, was palpable.[318] "Without having realized it, we found that we had only written the introduction to the analysis of the present," Sánchez explains. "In no other field of study has the past had so much force in the present – or the present, if you like, so much force on the past."[319]

In peripheral regions where export commodity production and natural resource extraction predominated, Afro-Colombians, indigenous people, and frontier settlers lived under limitless terror – during *la Violencia* and again at the end of the twentieth century.[320] Eventually, this was true for those living in the coffee axis, where many tactics were pioneered in the 1950s. The spread of contract killing, kidnapping, and extortion gave rise to a historical sense of tragic circularity and repetition. For many, hope for a better future was hard to sustain, and grounds for deep pessimism existed. This is the vacuum into which Álvaro Uribe stepped.

Right-wing repression and overgrown armed resistance explained the relative weakness and fragmentation of Colombia's radical-popular movements. Looking back, it is clear that whenever Colombia's political center tilted toward redistribution – of wealth, resources, political power – or peace negotiations with insurgents, it shifted right. Political power remained tied to landed wealth and control of territory. The enterprises of paramilitarized narcotics capos became more inclusive, better organized, and tightly linked to official politics after the mid-1990s. The narcotics business no longer depended on centralized cartels, and it united town and country far more than any other industry. No fraction of the Colombian oligarchy had brought other groups together around a project for hegemony at the national level. None led or directed other factions in strengthening the nation state, property rights, and command of labor. As a result, in the early twenty-first century, narco-paramilitaries – the private defenders of the state and private property – increasingly set the boundaries of local, regional, and even national elections.

The dispersed power from a weak political center attested to the parcellization of sovereignty. Yet if past precedent were anything to go by, emulation of Venezuelan counterinsurgency success in Falcón in the early 1960s, or Fujimori's in Ayacucho and the Upper Huallaga Valley in the 1990s, would require a capacity to mobilize a peasant constituency, both hostile to the guerrillas and amenable to anti-communist cliente-lism. This has never existed in the jungles and tropical plains of southern and southeastern Colombia. It remains to be seen whether the arrival of the Colombian Army, either preceded or followed by paramilitary occupation, will create one. Scorching the earth from the air, to render economic life impossible in rebel zones, is a tactic with antecedents in the early cold war. It evokes the terrible slogan coined by Zuleta in the epigraph to Chapter 7: "If we cannot and do not want to modify the circumstances that determine these manifestations of misery, margin-alization and despair, then let us eliminate the victims." Nevertheless, a strategy along these lines had not altered the first condition of the insurgencies and radical-popular mobilization – an exclusionary political order. It may have armor-plated it further.

Though Colombia is today exceptional within Latin America, thanks to its ongoing civil war, in the world at large it may be more repre-sentative than, say, Bolivia, where national-popular mobilization has set sharp limits on state violence, and led to the nationalization of hydro-carbon resources, as well as a shift in political representation away from the ruling minority of *criollos* and mestizos. I have focused on explaining the exceptional character of Colombia's political violence since the 1940s, but the final chapter suggests that under presidents Bush and Uribe, Colombia may have become a model for "successful" counter-insurgency and "low-intensity" democracies worldwide.

With the blessing of Washington and international financial institutions, in the 1990s wealth and power were concentrated to an extraordinary degree by exclusionary parliamentary democratic systems, characterized by regular elections, and neoliberal economic policies. El Salvador, Nicaragua, and Guatemala would be examples from the Latin American region where skyrocketing crime, impunity, and shadowy mafia-political murders followed "successful" counterinsurgency, except that the FMLN and the FSLN successfully endured, albeit in almost unrecognizable form, the transition from army to electoral party.[321] Like many "emerging market democracies" outside the North Atlantic, they feature endemic class and ethnic-racial conflict, high levels of violence and impunity, and a potent fusion of politics with organized crime. Iraq and Afghanistan would be other examples of societies where insurgencies, neoliberal economic policies, and "democratic" elections take place in the midst of growing impunity for organized crime, except that both are under US occupation, and are therefore exceptional.

As part of liberal nation state formation, other "low-intensity democracies" in Latin America established official Truth Commissions following periods of US government-sponsored state terror.[322] In the Colombian case, incorporation of paramilitaries into elections and public life – the fusion of politics and organized crime – is premised on officially enforced amnesia with precedents in the cold war. Through the Justice and Peace Law, Álvaro Uribe has allowed parastate criminals to bury their crimes in a haze of oblivion, and to prosper after the fashion of those amnestied by Rojas Pinilla in the 1950s.

There are at least three significant differences between then and now. First, lacking patronage ties to either party, Left insurgencies have little chance of partaking of the amnesty; under Uribe, the FARC, at least, will be targeted for elimination as "terrorists." Second, the regional coalition of paramilitary blocs is far stronger in relation to the two parties and the central government than it had been fifty years before. Its strategy of capital accumulation and its evolution as a parastate give it a considerable degree of relative autonomy from the state that created it. Third, the bipartisan system is collapsing under the impact of *uribismo*. Whatever its future, the Liberal-Conservative diarchy is unlikely to survive intact the proposed paramilitary integration into state and society.

Bringing an analysis of the past to bear on the present, I have situated public debates about memory and justice in light of what came before.

Colonial modes of political domination, economic exploitation, and racial/ethnic discrimination did not end with the Wars of Independence, but entered a new stage from which they have yet to emerge. The current moment is surely one of Colombia's darkest, but if the past is any guide, it, too, shall pass.

Radical-popular movements have proven to be nothing if not resilient, recreating themselves in extraordinarily difficult circumstances, despite successive waves of state, parastate, and even insurgent terror. They have struggled to hold the state accountable to its citizens, and to strengthen the rule of law according to constitutional rights. They have therefore offered a different model of authority – rooted in non-liberal, collective forms of democracy – than the state or the insurgencies, not to speak of the parastate. Compared to the Nasa in Cauca, the Peace Community of San José, or Afro-Colombian and indigenous communities in the Chocó, the FARC and the counterinsurgency have impoverished, militarist visions of democracy, security, autonomy, and sovereignty. Surveying the Colombian past, we might draw hope from the fact that, time and again, radical-popular movements have arisen to demand self-determination in a more peaceful, equitable, and just polity.

Notes

Introduction: Remembering Colombia

1 For statistics on the Chocó, see Grace Livingstone, *Inside Colombia: Drugs, Democracy, and War* (New Brunswick, NJ 2004), p. 75. For the history of the extraction of natural resources in the Chocó in the 1970s and 1980s, see Peter Wade, *Blackness and Race Mixture: The Dynamics of Racial Identity* (Baltimore, MD 1993), pp. 131–48. For racial categories such as mestizo and black, see *ibid.*, pp. 8–28. A note on statistics: I assume that they are part of political contests to define truth, rather than neutral numerical abstractions, and use them less for the sake of precision than for purposes of illustration.

2 For figures on US military and police aid to Colombia, see Adam Isaacson, "Number Three No More," 19 April 2005: www.ciponline.org.

3 "No en nuestros territorios," 15 November 2005: www.codhes.co; for English translations, see Adam Isaacson, " 'Not in our territories,' say Chocó leaders," www.ciponline.org.

4 Jon Wiener, "Mike Davis talks about the 'Heroes of Hell'," *Radical History Review* 85 (2003), pp. 227–37.

5 Antonio Caballero, "Infiltrados o reinsertados?" *Semana*, 30 April 2006.

6 For the concept of enclave economies, see Fernando Henrique Cardoso and Enzo Faletto, *Dependency and Development in Latin America* (Berkeley, CA 1979 [1971]), p. xix: "In enclave economies, foreign invested capital *originates in the exterior*, is incorporated into local productive processes, and transforms parts of itself into wages and taxes. Its value is increased by the exploitation of local labor forces, which transform nature and produce goods that realize again the life of this capital when staples (oil, copper, bananas, etc.) are sold in the *external market*." Italics in original. For critical discussion, see Catherine LeGrand, "Living in Macondo: Economy and Culture in a United Fruit Company Banana Enclave in Colombia," in Gilbert M. Joseph, Catherine C. LeGrand, and Ricardo D. Salvatore, eds, *Close Encounters of Empire: Writing the History of US-Latin American Relations* (Durham, NC 1998), pp. 334–7.

7 Iván Orozco Abad, "La democracia y el tratamiento del enemigo interior," *Análisis Político* 6 (Enero–Abril 1989), pp. 54–79.

8 Figures taken from Human Rights Watch, "Colombia: Resúmen de país," January 2006: www.hrw.org. On displacement, see Nora Segura Escobar, "Colombia: Guerra y desplazamiento forzoso," *Análisis Político* 43 (Mayo–Agosto 2001), pp. 85–106. On gender and displacement, see Donny Meertens, "Victims and Survivors of War in Colombia: Three Views of Gender Relations," in Charles Bergquist et al., eds, *Violence in Colombia, 1990–2000: Waging War and Negotiating Peace* (Wilmington, DE 2001), pp. 151–70; for bibliography, see Flor Alba Romero, "Población desplazada por la violencia en Colombia y otros países," *Análisis Político* 34 (Mayo–Agosto 1998), pp. 126–43.

9 For issues of justice, reparations, and reconciliation, see Iván Orozco Abad, "La posguerra colombiana," *Análisis Político* 46 (Mayo–Agosto 2002), pp. 78–99.

10 Human Rights Watch, "Colombia: Resúmen de país."

11 As elsewhere in Latin America, racial categories in Colombia are fluid, and self-identification shifts according to political processes and outcomes. According to the Colombian government's human rights observatory, roughly one in four Colombians was of African descent, while according to the former governor of the Chocó, Luis Gilberto Murillo, the true figure was between 36 and 40 per cent. Some 80 to 85 indigenous peoples represented an estimated 800,000 to 1 million people, perhaps 2 per cent of a national population of 44 million, according to the National Organization of Indigenous Colombians and the UN High Commission for Human Rights. See Luis Gilberto Murillo, "El Chocó: The African Heart of Colombia," *Colombia Update: Colombia Human Rights Network* (Winter/Spring 2001), pp. 12–13.

12 For the concept of internal colonialism in Colombia and Latin America, see Wade, *Blackness and Race Mixture*, pp. 147–8; *idem, Race and Ethnicity in Latin America* (London 1997), pp. 64–7. Schematically speaking, social formations structured by internal colonialism reproduce, often in new forms, relations of violence, domination, and exploitation derived from colonialism. In Latin America, the small minority at the top – where wealth and political power are more concentrated than in any other region in the world – is almost exclusively creole (of Spanish descent), while thin middle sectors generally adhere to the creole ideal whatever their hue. The majority of rural and urban laborers are dark-skinned descendants of Africans, indigenous groups, and people of mixed European-African-Native American descent (mestizos).

13 See Willian F. Sharp, *Slavery on the Spanish Frontier: The Colombian Chocó, 1680–1810* (Norman, OK 1976).

14 See Roland Marchal and Christine Messiant, "Las guerras civiles en la era de la globalización: nuevos conflictos y nuevos paradigmas," in *Análisis Político* 50 (Enero–Abril 2004), pp. 20–34. For a look at Colombia compared to

Italy, Lebanon, and Angola, see Nazih Richani, *Systems of Violence: The Political Economy of War and Peace in Colombia* (Albany, NY 2002), pp. 157–71.

15 A significant number of major historical and social scientific works are not cited below. I make no claim to comprehensiveness; since my task is essentially interpretive, I cite only works of which I have made use. Nonspecialists interested in reading more should consult the bibliographic essays in David Bushnell, *The Making of Modern Colombia: A Nation in Spite of Itself* (Berkeley, CA 1993); Frank Safford and Marco Palacios, *Colombia: Divided Land, Fragmented Society* (Oxford 2001); and Ricardo Peñaranda, "The War on Paper: A Balance Sheet on Works Published in the 1990s," in Charles Bergquist et al., eds, *Violence in Colombia: 1990–2000*, pp. 179–94.

16 Gonzalo Sánchez, "Guerra prolongada y negociaciones inciertas en Colombia," in Sánchez and Eric Lair, comps, *Violencias y estrategias colectivas en la región andina* (Bogotá 2004), p. 19.

17 The characterization of the conflict is the subject of ongoing debate. I follow three scholars of Colombian rural life: William Ramírez Tobón, "¿Guerra civil en Colombia?" *Análisis Político* 46 (Mayo–Agosto 2002), pp. 151–63; Darío Fajardo, "La internacionalización de la guerra," in Jairo Estrada Álvarez, comp., *El Plan Colombia y la intensificación de la guerra: Aspectos globales y locales* (Bogotá 2002), p. 71; Alfredo Molano, "¿Neutralidad?" *El Espectador*, 8 May 2005. See also, Alfredo Rángel, "Guerra civil de baja intensidad," *El Tiempo*, 23 May 2004.

18 Fernand Braudel, "History and the Social Sciences" (1958), in *On History*, trans. Sarah Matthews (Chicago 1980), p. 37; *idem*, "La historia operacional: La historia y la investigación del presente" (1971), *Contrahistorias* 2 (Mexico, DF), Marzo–Agosto 2004, pp. 29–40; Marc Bloch, *The Historians' Craft* (New York 1953), pp. 43–7; and E.H. Carr, *What is History?* (New York 1961), pp. 28–9, 35, 69. In Colombia, Darío Betancourt and Marta Luz García's work stressed this connection. See Daniel Pécaut, "Los aportes de Darío Betancourt Echeverry," in Gonzalo Sánchez et al., *Los intelectuales y la política* (Bogotá 2004), pp. 107–19. Betancourt was kidnapped and "disappeared" in 1999.

19 Alison Brysk, "Recovering from State Terror: The Morning After in Latin America," *Latin American Research Review* 38: 1 (February 2003), p. 239; Elizabeth Jelin, *State Repression and the Labors of Memory* (Minneapolis, MN 2003), pp. 46–9.

20 I refer to vulgar interpretations that posit a timeless, unchanging predilection for violence. While these interpretations prevail in policy-making circles, more historicized visions, like Álvaro Tirado Mejía's, stress the development of authoritarian educational institutions, political culture, and regulation of private life under the Regeneration and through *la Violencia* (1880–1964). These, of course, are worthy of serious consideration. See Fabio López de la Roche, "Cultura política de las clases dirigentes en

Colombia: Permanencias y rupturas," in López de la Roche, comp., *Ensayos sobre cultura política colombiana* (Bogotá 1990), pp. 119–20, n. 32.

21 James E. Sanders, *Contentious Republicans: Popular Politics, Race, and Class in Nineteenth-Century Colombia* (Durham, NC 2004), p. 197. Mary Roldán, *Blood and Fire: La Violencia in Antioquia, 1946–53* (Durham, NC 2002), p. 14. See also, Malcolm Deas, "Algunos interrogantes sobre la relación entre guerras civiles y violencia," in Gonzalo Sánchez and Ricardo Pañaranda, comps, *Pasado y presente de la Violencia en Colombia* (Bogotá 1986), pp. 41–6; and David Bushnell, "Politics and Violence in Nineteenth-Century Colombia," in Charles Bergquist et al., eds, *The Violence in Colombia: The Contemporary Crisis in Historical Perspective* (Wilmington, DE 1992), pp. 11–30.

22 Cardoso and Faletto, *Dependency and Development*, pp. 96–9; Tulio Halperín Donghi, *The Contemporary History of Latin America* (Durham, NC 1992 [1967]), p. 282, 383.

23 See Daniel Pécaut, *Orden y violencia: Colombia, 1930–53*, vol. I (Bogotá 1987), p. 18; Bushnell, *The Making of Modern Colombia*, p. 284; Marco Palacios, *Entre la legitimidad y la violencia: Colombia, 1875–1994* (Bogotá 1995), p. 237.

24 In addition to *The Prison Notebooks* (New York 1971 [1929–35]), my understanding of ruling-class hegemony and territorial fragmentation has been influenced by Antonio Gramsci, *The Southern Question* (West Lafayette, IN 1995), translated and introduced by Pasquale Verdicchio.

25 Following Catherine LeGrand, *Frontier Expansion and Peasant Protest in Colombia, 1850–1936* (Albuquerque, NM 1986), p. 207, I use the term "peasant" to refer to "small rural cultivators who rely on family labor to produce what they consume. Sharecroppers, service tenants, small proprietors, and frontier settlers would, by this definition, all be called peasants." Peasants are forced to pay tribute in foodstuffs, livestock, and, more often, money, to a range of state and religious officials and institutions.

26 Daniel James, *Resistance and Integration: Peronism and the Argentine Working Class, 1946–1976* (Cambridge 1988); Jeffrey Gould, *To Lead as Equals: Rural Protest and Political Consciousness in Chinandega, Nicaragua, 1912–1979* (Chapel Hill, NC 1990); Alan Knight, "Populism and Neo-Populism in Latin America, especially Mexico," *Journal of Latin American Studies* 30: 2 (May 1998), pp. 223–48; *idem*, "Revolutionary and Democratic Traditions in Latin America," *Bulletin of Latin American Research* 20: 2 (2001), pp. 147–86; Robert Whitney, *State and Revolution in Cuba: Mass Mobilization and Political Change, 1920–40* (Chapel Hill, NC 2001); Richard L. Turits, *Foundations of Despotism: Peasants, the Trujillo Regime, and Modernity in Dominican History* (Durham, NC 2004). Classic essays are Ernesto Laclau, *Politics and Ideology in Marxist Theory* (London 1982), pp. 143–98; and Carlos Vilas, "Latin American Populism: A Structural Approach," *Science and Society* 56: 4 (Winter 1992–93), pp. 389–420.

27 Jeremy Adelman's "Andean Impasses," *New Left Review* 18 (Nov/Dec 2002), pp. 41–72, depicts Peru and Venezuela as lacking populist traditions. As Fernando Coronil argues, in "Magical Illusions or Revolutionary

Magic? Chávez in Historical Context," *North American Congress on Latin America* 33: 6 (May/June 2000), the Chávez regime is best understood against the historical background of the petroleum populism of the 1970s. In the early 1970s, both the Velasco regime in Peru and the Pérez administration in Venezuela were populist – especially compared to Colombian President Misael Pastrana (1970–74). See Marco Palacios, "Presencia y ausencia populista: Un contrapunto colombo-venezolano," in *Análisis Político* 39 (Enero–Abril 2000), pp. 33–51.

28 Greg Grandin, *The Last Colonial Massacre: Latin America in the Cold War* (Chicago 2004), p. 188.

29 For primitive accumulation, see Karl Marx, *Capital*, vol. 1 (New York 1992 [1867]), pp. 871–940; David Harvey, *The New Imperialism* (Oxford 2003); Silvia Federici, *Caliban and the Witch* (New York 2004); Retort, *Afflicted Powers* (New York 2005); Mike Davis, *Planet of Slums* (New York 2006). While classical Marxism saw primitive accumulation as a stage in historical development that preceded the Industrial Revolution, it is more useful to think of it as a recurring feature of capitalist development in which labor power is created via the expropriation and privatization of lands, forests, and rivers that form the material basis of communal livelihoods.

30 Taken from Antonio Gramsci, "subaltern" has been defined in the context of the study of colonialism and nationalism in South Asia as "a name for the general attribute of subordination . . . whether this is expressed in terms of class, caste, age, gender and office or in any other way . . . We recognize that of course that subordination cannot be understood except as one of the constitutive terms in a binary relationship of which the other is dominance." Ranajit Guha, "Preface," *Subaltern Studies I: Writing of South Asian History and Society* (Delhi 1982), p. vii. I use it to capture the heterogeneity of subordinate groups in Colombia.

31 In "La colonización de La Macarena en la historia de la frontera agrícola," in Alfredo Molano et al., *"Yo le digo unas cosas": La colonización de la reserva Macarena* (Bogotá 1989), p. 203, Darío Fajardo named this the "violence-migration-colonization-violence" cycle of conflict.

32 As sketched in Barrington Moore, *The Social Origins of Dictatorship and Democracy* (Boston, MA 1969), pp. 437–8.

33 Palacios, *Entre la legitimidad y la violencia*, p. 280.

34 Moore, *The Social Origins of Dictatorship and Democracy*, p. 215.

35 I borrow the former phrase from Perry Anderson, *Passages from Antiquity to Feudalism* (London 1974), p. 148; and the latter from Sánchez, "Guerra prolongada y negociaciones inciertas en Colombia," p. 58.

Radical-Popular Republicanism, 1848–80

36 "Atlantic republican democracies" refers to polities in the USA, Europe, and Latin America. See Eric Hobsbawm, *The Age of Capital, 1848–75* (New York 1975).

37 Malcolm Deas, "The Fiscal Problems of Nineteenth-Century Colombia," *Journal of Latin American Studies* 14: 2 (1982), pp. 287–328.

38 M. Samper, *La miseria de Bogotá* (Bogotá 1867), cited in Pécaut, *Orden y violencia*, p. 33.

39 Pécaut, *Orden y violencia*, pp. 29–37.

40 James Payne, *Patterns of Conflict in Colombia* (New Haven, CT 1968), pp. 121–2.

41 Daniel Pécaut, *Guerra contra la sociedad* (Bogotá 2001), pp. 56–7; Bushnell, *The Making of Modern Colombia*, p. 126. With the possible exception of Mexico or Uruguay, identification with political parties did not run as deep anywhere else in the region.

42 For the process by which Antioquia became Conservative, see Nancy Appelbaum, *Muddied Waters: Race, Region, and Local History in Colombia, 1846–1948* (Durham, NC 2003), pp. 45–7. For Liberal predominance on the Atlantic coast, see Helen Delpar, *Red Against Blue: The Liberal Party in Colombian Politics, 1863–99* (Alabama 1981), pp. 16–21; Eduardo Posada Carbó, *The Colombian Caribbean: A Regional History, 1870–1950* (Oxford 1996), pp. 235–51.

43 Frank Safford and Marco Palacios, *Colombia: Fragmented Land, Divided Society* (Oxford 2001), pp. 115, 126, 142, 151, 204.

44 "Diario Histórico del Ejército Unido de Antioquia e Cauca," in James Sanders, *Contentious Republicans*, p. 120.

45 This is compable to the US experience after Reconstruction, in which an assault on Native and African American liberties, rights, and communities was waged in the name of agro-industrial "progress." See Nell Irvin Painter, *Standing at Armageddon: The United States, 1877–1916* (New York 1988).

From Reaction to Rebellion, 1880–1930

46 For racial formation and the racialization of Antioquia and Cauca after 1880, see Appelbaum, *Muddied Waters*, pp. 31–51. For Antioquia, the Chocó, and the Atlantic coast, see Wade, *Blackness and Race Mixture*, pp. 66–105.

47 The preceding paragraphs summarize Chapters 3–6 of Sanders, *Contentious Republicans*, pp. 58–183. The quotation appears on p. 184.

48 Gonzalo Sánchez, "Intelectuales . . . Poder . . . Cultura Nacional," in Sánchez et al., *Los intelectuales y la política*, pp. 60–65; Malcolm Deas, *El poder y la gramática* (Bogotá 1993). See also, Miguel Ángel Urrego, "La noción de la ciudadanía bajo la Regeneración: Colombia, 1880–1900," in Rossana Barragán et al., comps, *El Siglo XIX: Bolivia y América Latina* (La Paz 1997), pp. 651–62.

49 Also a grammarian, Suárez authored *Sueños gramaticales de Luciano Pulgar* (Bogotá 1966 [1923]). For the War of a Thousand Days, see Charles Bergquist, *Coffee and Conflict in Colombia: Origins and Outcome of the War of a Thousand Days, 1886–1910* (Durham, NC 1978).

50 Bergquist, "La guerra popular en la Guerra de los Mil Días," *Análisis Político* 52 (Septiembre–Diciembre 2004), pp. 77–89.

51 In Marxist terms, surplus was mainly extracted at the point of exchange rather than production, as noted in *idem*, "The Labor Movement in Colombia (1930–1946)," in Bergquist et al., eds, *Violence in Colombia: Historical Perspective*, p. 68.

52 Michael Jiménez, *Struggles on an Interior Shore*, forthcoming.

53 Mario Arango, *Café e Industria 1850–1930* (Bogotá 1977); Absalón Machado, *El café: de la aparcería al capitalismo* (Bogotá 1977); Charles Bergquist, *Coffee and Conflict in Colombia, 1886–1910* (Durham, NC 1978); Marco Palacios, *Coffee in Colombia: An Economic, Social, and Political History* (London 1980); Michael Jiménez, "Traveling Far in Grandfather's Car: The Life Cycle of Central Colombian Coffee Estates: The Case of Viotá, 1900–30," *Hispanic American Historical Review* 69: 2 (1989), pp. 185–219; *idem*, "At the Banquet of Civilization: The Limits of Planter Hegemony in Early Twentieth-Century Colombia," in William Roseberry et al., eds, *Coffee, Society, and Power in Latin America* (Baltimore, MD 1995), pp. 262–93.

54 Because of the spread of property ownership, mid-twentieth-century North American social scientists and Antioquian exceptionalists hailed *paisa*-led coffee capitalism as a process of democratic capitalist modernization. See James Parsons, *Antioqueño Colonization in Western Colombia* (Berkeley, CA 1949); William Paul McGreevy, *An Economic History of Colombia, 1845–1930* (Cambridge 1971); Keith Christie, "Antioqueño Colonization in Western Colombia: A Reappraisal," *Hispanic American Historical Review* 58: 2 (May 1978), pp. 260–63; Ann Twinam, *Miners, Merchants, and Farmers in Colonial Colombia* (Austin, TX 1982), pp. 20–21.

55 Ann Farnsworth-Alvear, *Dulcinea in the Factory: Medellín's Industrial Experiment, 1900–1950* (Durham, NC 2000).

56 Sánchez, "Intelectuales . . . Poder . . . Cultura Nacional," pp. 68–9; Fabio López de la Roche, "Cultura política de las clases dirigentes en Colombia," p. 111. See also, Frank Safford, *The Ideal of the Practical: Colombia's Struggle to Form a Technical Elite* (Austin, TX 1976); Alberto Mayor Mora, *Ética, trabajo, productividad en Antioquia* (Bogotá 1984); Pamela Murray, "Engineering Development: Colombia's School of Mines, 1887–1930," *Hispanic American Historical Review* 74: 1 (1994), pp. 63–82.

57 Appelbaum, *Muddied Waters*, pp. 33–40.

58 Mario Arango, *Los funerales de Antioquia la grande* (Medellín 1990); Fernando Botero Herrera, *Medellín, 1890–1950: Historia urbana y juego de intereses* (Medellín 1996); Michael F. Jiménez, "'From Plantation to Cup:' Coffee and Capitalism in the United States, 1830–1930," in Roseberry et al., eds, *Coffee, Society, and Power in Latin America*, pp. 38–64.

59 Vernon Lee Fluharty, *Dance of the Millions: Military Rule and the Social Revolution in Colombia* (Pittsburgh, PA 1957); Paul Drake, *The Money Doctor in the Andes: The Kemmerer Missions, 1923–33* (Durham, NC 1989);

Charles Bergquist, "The Labor Movement (1930–46) and the Origins of the Violence," p. 57.

60 Roldán, *Blood and Fire*, p. 31.

61 Brooke Larson, *Trials of Nation-Making: Liberalism, Race, and Ethnicity in the Andes, 1810–1910* (Cambridge 2004), p. 252.

62 Joanne Rappaport, *The Politics of Memory: Native Historical Interpretation in the Colombian Andes*, 2nd edn (Durham, NC 1998), p. 114.

63 Gary Long, "The Dragon Finally Came: Industrial Capitalism, Radical Artisans and the Liberal Party in Colombia, 1910–1948," Ph.D. Thesis, University of Pittsburgh (1995).

64 Eduardo Posada Carbó, "Fiction as History: The *bananeras* and Gabriel García Márquez's *One Hundred Years of Solitude*," *Journal of Latin American Studies* 30: 2 (1998), pp. 395–414. Marco Palacios notes the lack of consensus over the exact number massacred: the North American consul put the figure at 1,000, the strike leader Alberto Castrillón at 1,500, and the general in charge of the massacre at 47; see *Entre la legitimidad y la violencia*, p. 120. David Bushnell, citing Roberto Herrera Soto and Rafael Romero Castañeda, considers the number of 60 to 75 "definitive:" *The Making of Modern Colombia*, p. 180.

65 See W. John Green, *Gaitanismo, Left Liberalism and Popular Mobilization in Colombia* (Gainesville, FL 2003).

66 Herbert Braun, *The Assassination of Gaitán: Public Life and Urban Violence in Colombia* (Madison, WI 1986), pp. 8–9, 45–6, 54–5. Braun contends that *gaitanismo* had little impact on organized labour, but Green has shown otherwise.

67 Gonzalo Sánchez, "Los bolsheviques de Líbano," in *Ensayos de historia social y política del siglo XX*, pp. 11–111.

The Liberal Pause, 1930–46

68 W. John Green, "Sibling Rivalry on the Left and Labor Struggles in Colombia during the 1940s," *Latin American Research Review* 35: 1 (2000), pp. 93, 115.

69 For Latin America's extraordinary democratic opening between 1944 and 1946, before the deep freeze set in after 1948, see Leslie Bethell and Ian Roxborough, eds, *Latin America between the Second World War and the Cold War, 1944–1948* (Cambridge 1992); Grandin, *The Last Colonial Massacre*, p. 176.

70 Sánchez, "Las Ligas Campesinas en Colombia," in *Ensayos de historia social y política*, pp. 152–68.

71 Marc Chernick and Michael Jiménez, "Popular Liberalism, Radical Democracy, and Marxism: Leftist Politics in Contemporary Colombia, 1974–1991," in Barry Carr and Steven Ellner, eds, *The Latin American Left: From the Fall of Allende to Perestroika* (Boulder, CO 1993), p. 66.

72 In the Third Period of the Communist International (1928–35), commu-

nist parties were instructed by Stalin and the Soviet bureaucracy to compete with other organizations on the Left and to avoid cross-class coalitions. See C.L.R. James, *The Rise and Fall of World Revolution: The Third International, 1919–36* (London 1937). For the foundation of the Communist International, see E.H. Carr, *The Bolshevik Revolution, 1917–1923*, vol. 3 (New York 1953).

73 For a skeptical view, see Richard Stoller, "Alfonso López Pumarejo and Liberal Radicalism in 1930s Colombia," *Journal of Latin American Studies* 27 (1995), pp. 367–97.

74 In contrast to the Third Period, during the Popular Front (1935–39), Stalin and the Soviet bureaucracy ordered communist parties to ally themselves with bourgeois reformers and competitors on the Left, in the name of unity against fascism.

75 Richani, *Systems of Violence*, pp. 20–23.

76 Charles Bergquist, "The Labor Movement (1930–46) and the Origins of the Violence," pp. 52, 62, 69–70. A similar interpretation is offered by Christopher Abel and Marco Palacios, "Colombia: 1930–58," in Leslie Bethell, ed., *The Cambridge History of Latin America*, vol. 8 (Cambridge 1991), p. 592.

77 Michael Jiménez, "The Many Deaths of the Colombian Revolution," *Columbia Papers on Latin America* 13 (1990); Green, "Sibling Rivalry on the Left," pp. 99–112.

78 See Medófilo Medina, "Violence and Economic Development: 1945–50 and 1985–88," in Bergquist et al., *Violence in Colombia: Historical Perspective*, pp. 157–8; Pécaut, *Guerra contra la sociedad*, pp. 58–9; and Eduardo Sáenz Rovner, *La ofensiva empresarial: Industriales, políticos, y violencia en los años 40 en Colombia* (Bogotá 1992).

79 Green, "Sibling Rivalry on the Left," p. 103.

80 This point is cogently argued by Pécaut in *Orden y violencia*, pp. 286–302.

81 For a vivid account of these events and their background, see James Henderson, *Modernization in Colombia. The Laureano Gómez Years, 1889–1965* (Gainesville, FL 2001), pp. 183–9.

82 The notion of the defensive feud was developed in Payne, *Patterns of Conflict in Colombia*, pp. 161–7.

83 W. John Green, " 'Vibrations of the Collective': The Popular Ideology of Gaitanismo on Colombia's Atlantic Coast, 1944–48," *Hispanic American Historical Review* 76: 2 (1996), pp. 283–311.

La Violencia, 1946–57

84 Gonzalo Sánchez, *Guerra y política en la sociedad colombiana* (Bogotá 1991), p. 31.

85 Bergquist, "The Labor Movement," pp. 60–61.

86 Roldán, *Blood and Fire*, pp. 22–9, provides a concise overview of the literature, which is far too vast for full citation. Two classic studies deserve

mention, however: Orlando Fals Borda, Germán Guzmán, and Eduardo Umaña Luna, *La Violencia en Colombia* (Bogotá 1962), the impact of which triggered congressional debate; and Paul Oquist, *Violencia, conflicto, y política en Colombia* (Bogotá 1978), which argued that *la Violencia* resulted from a "partial collapse of the state," stimulating new avenues of research.

87 There, agrarian struggle from the 1910s through the 1940s was individualized and local, whereas in Tolima and Cundinamarca it was collective and trans-local. Darío Betancourt and Marta Luz García, *Matones y cuadrilleros: Origen y evolución de la violencia en el occidente colombiano, 1946–65* (Bogotá 1990), pp. 19, 23–4, 177.

88 Gonzalo Sánchez, *Los días de la Revolución: Gaitanismo y 9 de abril en la provincia* (Bogotá 1983).

89 *Idem*, "The Violence: An Interpretive Synthesis," in Bergquist et al., eds, *Violence in Colombia*, pp. 77, 81–3.

90 Quoted in Robin Kirk, *More Terrible than Death: Massacres, Drugs, and America's War in Colombia* (New York 2003), p. 21.

91 Briefly, substitutionism can be defined as the notion that an organized vanguard party or army can make a revolution irrespective of the weakness of peasant and working-class movements.

92 See Antonio García, *Gaitanismo y el problema de la revolución colombiana* (Bogotá 1955).

93 Sánchez, "The Violence: An Interpretive Synthesis," pp. 83–6.

94 The contrast with Chile is instructive: there, communists were driven out of the countryside, and, from 1948, oriented strategy toward urban trade unions and slums.

95 Medófilo Medina, "La resistencia campesina en el sur de Tolima," in Sánchez and Peñaranda, comps, *Pasado y presente de la Violencia en Colombia*, pp. 233–65.

96 Betancourt and García, *Matones y cuadrilleros*, pp. 76–127.

97 Sánchez, "The Violence: An Interpretive Synthesis," pp. 88–9.

98 *Idem, Guerra y política*, pp. 31–2.

99 *Idem*, "Raíces de la amnistía o las etapas de la guerra en Colombia," in *Ensayos de historia social y política*, pp. 215–75; Alfredo Molano, *Amnistía y Violencia* (Bogotá 1978).

100 Kirk, *More Terrible than Death*, pp. 26–7, from María Victoria Uribe, *Matar, rematar, contramatar: Las masacres de la Violencia en el Tolima, 1948–64* (Bogotá 1996); see also, Fals Borda, Guzmán, and Umaña, *La Violencia en Colombia*.

101 José Alvear Restrepo was a "people's lawyer" and radical thinker, whose legacy has been honored by the lawyers' collective that bears his name.

102 Sánchez, "The Violence: An Interpretive Synthesis," pp. 95–7; *idem, Guerra y política en la sociedad*, pp. 39–42.

103 See Henderson, *Modernization in Colombia*, pp. 366, 370.

104 See Eduardo Pizarro, *Las FARC: De la autodefensa a la combinación de todas las formas de lucha* (Bogotá 1991); Alfredo Molano, *Selva Adentro* (Bogotá

1987), pp. 36–48; and *idem, Trochas y Fusiles* (Bogotá 1994), pp. 91–103; for Sumapaz, see José Jairo González Arias and Elsy Marulanda, *Historias de frontera: Colonización y guerras en el Sumapaz* (Bogotá 1990); for the prehistory, see Michael Jiménez, "Gender, Class, and the Roots of Peasant Resistance in Central Colombia, 1900–1930," in Forrest Colburn, ed., *Everyday Forms of Peasant Resistance* (New York 1990), pp. 121–50.

105 See Charles Bergquist, *Labor in Latin America: Comparative Essays on Chile, Argentina, Venezuela, and Colombia* (Stanford, CA 1986), pp. 276, 296, 312–14; and *idem*, "The Labor Movement (1930–46) and the Violence," in Bergquist et al., eds, *Violence in Colombia: Historical Perspective*, pp. 51–72.

106 In this, Colombia was hardly unusual. Eric Hobsbawm argues that one of the distinguishing features of European warfare in the twentieth, as compared to the nineteenth, century was the absence of limits, the deliberate targeting of the civilian population, and the recrudescence of torture. Eric Hobsbawm, *The Age of Empire: 1876–1913* (New York 1987); and *idem, The Age of Extremes: The Short Twentieth Century, 1914–1991* (New York 1992). For a sober assessment of nineteenth-century wars in Colombia and Europe, see Mauricio Romero, *Paramilitares y autodefensas, 1982–2003* (Bogotá 2003), pp. 51–3.

107 Catherine LeGrand, "Agrarian Antecedents of the Violence," in Bergquist et al., eds, *Violence in Colombia: Historical Perspective*, pp. 31–50; Gonzalo Sánchez and Donny Meertens, *Bandoleros, gamonales, y campesinos: El caso de la Violencia en Colombia* (Bogotá 1983).

108 Betancourt and García, *Matones y cuadrilleros*, p. 64.

The National Front: Political Lockout, 1957–82

109 Sánchez, *Guerra y política en la sociedad colombiana*, pp. 222–3; *idem*, "Intelectuales . . . Poder . . . Cultura Nacional," p. 84.

110 Álvaro Tirado Mejía, "Introducción," in *Nueva Historia de Colombia*, vol. 1 (Bogotá 1989), p. xi.

111 Francisco Leal Buitrago and Andrés Dávila, *Clientelismo: El sistema político y su expresión regional* (Bogotá 1994).

112 In Colombia alone, liberation theology was opposed by the Church hierarchy en bloc (excepting Gerardo Valencia Cano, Bishop of Buenaventura), and those who chose to pursue its path, by and large, wound up dead, in exile, or, like the Spaniards Manuel Pérez, Domingo Laín and José Antonio Jiménez, swelling the meager *filas* of the ELN. See Walter J. Broderick, *El guerrillero invisible* (Bogotá 2000), p. 117.

113 Sánchez, "The Violence: An Interpretive Synthesis," pp. 110–11; *idem*, "Reseña: *Entre la legitimidad y la violencia*, por Marco Palacios," *Análisis Político* 27 (Enero–Abril 1996), p. 104.

114 Though Sánchez, *ibid.*, p. 84, refers to the effort to mold the state into "the right arm of the capitalist classes," how effective it was in protecting

148   FORREST HYLTON

bourgeois interests is open to question. Pécaut and others have argued convincingly that the Colombian state's ineffectiveness as a vehicle for advancing a unified, national bourgeois agenda led to the retrenchment of landed elites, and the proliferation of private violence in the regions.

115 *Ibid.*, p. 120.

116 Sánchez and Meertens, *Bandoleros, gamonales, y campesinos*; Betancourt and García, *Matones y cuadrilleros*, pp. 137–75. At first, "Desquite" had official protection from Liberal notables in the towns and landlords in the country-side, but eventually, both Desquite and Efraín González tightened private networks of extraction over coffee farms, which led to a war against their one-time protectors, and then against their support base. This was the characteristic pattern of political involution in Tolima, Viejo Caldas, and northern Valle del Cauca.

117 Palacios, *Entre la legitimidad y la violencia*, pp. 258, 261–2.

118 Francisco Leal Buitrago, *El oficio de la guerra: La seguridad nacional en Colombia* (Bogotá 1994).

119 *Idem*, "Defensa y seguridad nacional, 1958–93," in Francisco Leal and Juan Gabriel Tokatlian, comps, *Orden mundial y seguridad: Nuevos desfíos para Colombia y América Latina* (Bogotá 1994), pp. 131–72.

120 Albert O. Hirschman, "Land Use and Land Reform in Colombia," *Journeys Toward Progress: Studies in Economic Policy-Making in Latin America* (New York 1975 [1963]), pp. 102–103.

121 Quotations from Kirk, *More Terrible than Death*, pp. 47–50.

122 Sánchez, "The Violence: An Interpretive Synthesis", p. 117.

123 "Plan Link," or "Plan Latin American Security Operation" in English.

124 For an account written by a FARC strategist and ideologue, see Jacobo Arenas, "La resistencia de Marquetalia," in Olga Behar, comp., *Las guerras de la paz* (Bogotá 1986), pp. 68–74. See also, José Joaquín Matallana, "El operativo," in *ibid.*, pp. 74–7.

125 Pizarro Leongómez, "Revolutionary Guerrilla Groups," in Bergquist et al., eds, *Violence in Colombia: Historical Perspective*, pp. 181–2.

126 Torres, who studied with Peruvian Gustavo Gutiérrez at the Louvain in Belgium, inspired Gutiérrez's landmark text of 1967, *Liberation Theology*, as discussed in Penny Lernoux, *Cry of the People* (New York 1977), pp. 29–31. See Alfonso Ojeda Awad, "El E.L.N.," in Behar, comp., *Las guerras de la paz*, pp. 51–67; Carlos Medina Gallego, *ELN: una historia en dos voces contadas* (Bogotá 1996); Fabiola Calvo Ocampo, *Manuel Pérez: un cura español en la guerrilla colombiana* (Madrid 1998); Broderick, *El guerrillero invisible*.

127 For this group, see "Ernesto Rojas," "E.P.L.," in Behar, comp., *Las guerras de la paz*, pp. 43–50; Fabiola Calvo Ocampo, *EPL: una historia armada* (Madrid 1987); and Álvaro Villarraga and Nelson Plazas, *Para reconstruir los sueños: una historia del EPL* (Bogotá 1994). For Julio Guerra, see Jaime Zuluaga Nieto, "La metamorfosis de un guerrillero: De liberal a maoísta," *Análisis Político* 18 (Enero–Abril 1993), pp. 103–16.

128 "Antonio," in Behar, comp., *Las guerras de la paz*, pp. 270–71; Pizarro,

"Revolutionary Guerrilla Groups," in Bergquist et al., eds, *Violence in Colombia: Historical Perspective*, pp. 174–8.

129 Palacios, *Entre la legitimidad y la violencia*, p. 256; Pécaut, *Guerra contra la sociedad*, p. 77.

130 Leon Zamosc, *The Agrarian Question and the Peasant Movement in Colombia: Struggles of the National Peasant Association, 1967–1981* (Cambridge 1986); Silvia Rivera Cusicanqui, *The Politics and Ideology of the Colombian Peasant Movement: the Case of ANUC (National Association of Peasant Smallholders)* (Bogotá 1987).

131 Fernando Cubides, "From Private to Public Violence: The Paramilitaries," in Bergquist et al., eds, *Violence in Colombia, 1990–2000*, p. 131. Betancourt and García, *Matones y cuadrilleros*, p. 135.

132 Sutti Ortiz, *Uncertainties in Peasant Farming: A Colombian Case* (London 1973); CINEP (Centro de Investigación y Educación Popular), *Consejo Regional Indígena del Cauca-CRIC: Diez años de lucha, historia, y documentos* (Bogotá 1978); Cristian Gros, *Colombia Indígena: Identidad cultural y cambio social* (Bogotá 1991); Jasmin Hristov, "Indigenous Struggles for Land and Cultura in Cauca, Colombia," *Journal of Peasant Studies* 32: 1 (January 2005), pp. 88–117.

133 Palacios, *Entre la legitimidad y la violencia*, pp. 269–70.

134 Like Tirofijo, General Tovar considered that the Colombian oligarchy had committed a strategic error in launching Operation Marquetalia in 1964. Sánchez, "Guerra prolongada y negociaciones inciertas," pp. 41–2.

135 Eduardo Pizarro, "Elementos para una sociología de la guerrilla colombiana," in *Guerra en Colombia* (Bogotá 2004), p. 66.

136 Pierre Gilhodes, "Movimientos sociales en los años ochenta y noventa," in Álvaro Tirado Mejía, comp., *La Nueva Historia de Colombia*, vol. VIII (Bogotá 1995), pp. 171–90.

137 On torture under Turbay, see Behar, comp., *Las guerras de la paz*, pp. 165–88.

138 Sánchez, "Intelectuales . . . Poder . . . Cultura Nacional," pp. 54–5; Kirk, *More Terrible than Death*, p. 62.

139 On M-19, see Israel Santamaria in Behar, comp., *Las guerras de la paz*, pp. 78–86; Darío Villamizar, *Aquel 19 será* (Bogotá 1995); Laura Restrepo, *Historia de un entusiasmo* (Bogotá 1999); María Eugenia Vásquez Perdomo, *My Life as a Colombian Revolutionary: Reflections of a Former Guerrillera* (Philadephia 2005), trans. Lorena Terando.

140 Ana María Bejarano, "La violencia regional y sus protagonistas: El caso de Urabá," *Análisis Político* 4 (Mayo–Agosto 1988), pp. 56–70; Fernando Botero Herrera, *Urabá: Colonización, violencia, y crisis del Estado* (Medellín 1990); María Teresa Uribe, *Urabá: ¿Región o territorio?* (Medellín 1992); Clara Inés García, *Urabá: Región, actores y conflicto, 1960–1990* (Bogotá 1996); William Ramírez Tobón, *Urabá: Los inciertos confines de una crisis* (Bogotá 1997).

141 Darío Betancourt and Marta Luz García, *Contrabandistas, marimberos y*

mafiosos: Historia social de la mafia colombiana (1965–1992) (Bogotá 1994), p. 47.

142 On outlaw rentier capitalists, politics, and state formation in southern Italy and Sicily, see Pino Arlacchi, *Mafia Business: The Mafia Ethic and the Spirit of Capitalism* (London 1986). See also, Ciro Krauthausen, *Padrinos y mercaderes: Crimen organizado en Italia y Colombia* (Bogotá 1998).

Negotiating the Dirty War, 1982–90

143 In fact, the Medellín cartel was a series of overlapping, concentric circles; the links between them were contingent and frequently ephemeral. To avoid confusion, I stick to conventional usage.

144 Kirk, *More Terrible than Death*, p. 82.

145 Escobar and associates, such as his cousin, Gustavo "Osito" Gaviria, or "el Negro" Galeano, came from working-class neighborhoods in Envigado and had gained business-fighting experience in the Urabá tobacco wars of the early 1970s. The Medellín elite initially barred them from buying into industry, and refused them membership of their exclusive clubs. The Cali capos, who came from middle-class and upper middle-class backgrounds, were considerably more successful at discreetly integrating themselves into the regional oligarchy, though Chepe Santacruz had to build his own club after being blackballed by the Club Colombia.

146 On Rodríguez, see Jorge Enrique Velásquez, "El Navegante," *Cómo me infiltré y engañé al Cartel* (Bogotá 1992).

147 Romero, *Paramilitares*, pp. 124–40; *idem*, "Democratización política y contrareforma paramilitar," in Sánchez and Lair, comps, *Violencias y estrategias colectivas*, pp. 337–76.

148 Molano, *Selva Adentro*, p. 100.

149 Romero, *Paramilitares*, pp. 339, 345, 373.

150 Palacios, *Entre la legitimidad y la violencia*, p. 275.

151 In 1989, along with Oliver North, Maj. Gen. Richard Secord, former National Security Advisor John Poindexter, and former CIA station chief in Costa Rica Joseph Fernandez, former Ambassador Tambs was declared persona non grata in Costa Rica under the country's Nobel Peace Prize-winning president, Arturo Arias. As Ambassador, Tambs coordinated and covered up for the Nicaraguan Contra – an irregular counterinsurgent force financed by the narcotics business. Luis A. Restrepo, "The Equivocal Dimensions of Human Rights in Colombia," in Bergquist et al., eds, *Violence in Colombia, 1990–2000*, p. 102.

152 Richani, *Systems of Violence*, p. 182, n. 7. Betancur offended the high command by appointing a general from the Air Force to head the Armed Forces, and trying to diminish the Army's power over the police.

153 For the shifting geography of narcotics production and anti-communist counterinsurgency in the cold war, beginning with CIA support for the

Corsican mafia on the docks of Marseille, and Chinese nationalists on the Burmese border of Yunnan, China, see Alfred W. McCoy, *The Politics of Heroin: CIA Complicity in the Global Drug Trade* (New York 1991). What is interesting for our purposes is that in Colombia, landlords funded rural counterinsurgency, on a much lower scale, decades before the drug business became its driving economic force.

154 See Ana Carrigan, *The Palace of Justice: A Colombian Tragedy* (New York 1994); for a survivor's account, see Humberto Murica Ballén, "Palacio en llamas," in Behar, comp., *Las guerras de la paz*, pp. 405–13.

155 The FARC's XI Front, characterized by arbitrary violence, kidnapping, and unbearably high levels of taxation, had created a climate of hostility in which the armed forces and paramilitaries were able to obtain the collaboration of those in the civilian population most opposed to FARC exactions. See Medina Gallego, *Autodefensas, paramilitares, y narcotráfico en Colombia: Origin, desarrollo y consolidación: el caso "Puerto Boyacá"* (Bogotá 1990), pp. 142–7.

156 *Ibid.*, pp. 159–66. Curiously, this chapter of counterinsurgency is overlooked in Charles Bergquist, "Waging War and Negotiating Peace: The Contemporary Crisis in Historical Perspective," in Bergquist et al., eds, *Violence in Colombia, 1990–2000*, p. 208; and Daniel Pécaut, *Guerra contra la sociedad*, pp. 300–305.

157 *Ibid.*, pp. 163, 232–3; also, Alejandro Reyes Posada, "Paramilitares en Colombia: Contexto, aliados y consecuencias," *Análisis Político* 12 (Enero–Abril 1991), pp. 35–41; *idem*, "Propiedad de la tierra y narcotráfico en Colombia," in Álvaro Tirado Mejía, comp., *La Nueva Historia de Colombia*, vol. VIII (Bogotá 1995), pp. 23–33; Cubides, "From Private to Public Violence," in Bergquist et al., eds, *Violence in Colombia, 1990–2000*, pp. 127–49.

158 Yanine went back to the School of the Americas after his triumph in the Magdalena Medio – as a guest speaker. He was later convicted of planning a 1988 massacre of twenty banana workers in Urabá. Garry Leech, *Killing Peace: Colombia's Conflict and the Failure of US Intervention* (New York 2001), p. 27.

159 I disagree with Alfred Molano, "Fórmulas," *El Espectador*, 15 September 2002, who argues that it was a "wise" strategy. Though it is not easy to spell out a viable alternative, the FARC might have applied the tight security measures the situation demanded, protecting their people and allies in the UP from needless risk. "When they started murdering us, we all asked ourselves, 'Why didn't they give us military training?'" As a former UP militant put it, "'We're being killed and what are they doing?' Nothing was the answer." Steven Dudley, *Walking Ghosts: Murder and Guerrilla Politics in Colombia* (New York 2004), p. 133.

160 This faction is currently dominant within the FARC's Estado Mayor, and is best represented by Jorge Briceño, a.k.a. "Mono Jojoy," the FARC's military commander.

161 This is the argument of Dudley's *Walking Ghosts*, which provides an in-depth look at the debates that divided FARC hardliners (*los ortodoxos*) from radical social democrats (*los perestroikas*) grouped under UP banners.

162 Dudley, *Walking Ghosts*, p. 82.

163 *Ibid.*, p. 101. Though the feud between narcotraffickers and the guerrillas is usually chalked up to the kidnapping, which led to the formation of MAS, disputed profits from the cocaine business lay at the root of the dispute. Apparently, the FARC had stolen merchandise from Rodríguez Gacha at one of his largest cocaine laboratories, Tranquilandia, discovered in Meta by Colombian National Police and the DEA in 1984. The 13.8 metric tons of cocaine, estimated at $34 million, represented the largest bust in history. See Alonso Salazar, *La parábola de Pablo: Auge y caída de un gran capo de narcotráfico* (Bogotá 2002), p. 111; Kirk, *More Terrible than Death*, p. 86.

164 For *sicarios* and urban warfare in Medellín, see Alonso Salazar, *No Nacimos pa' Semilla* (Bogotá 1990); Carlos Miguel Ortiz Sarmiento, "El sicariato en Medellín: Entre la violencia política y el crimen organizado," *Análisis Político* 14 (Septiembre–Diciembre 1991), pp. 68–84; Ana María Jaramillo et al., *Cultura política y violencia en Medellín en los 90* (Medellín 1999); Ramiro Ceballos Melguizo, "The Evolution of Armed Conflict in Medellín: An Analysis of the Major Actors," *Latin American Perspectives* 28 (2001), pp. 110–31.

165 Horacio Serpa, "Guerra sucia, autodefensa y guerrilla," *Análisis Político* 2 (Marzo–Abril 1987), p. 140.

166 For testimony about the development of these practices during the early 1970s in the FARC's VII Front, the only one controlled by Jacobo Arenas, Manuel Marulanda, and the Estado Mayor, see "Antonio," in Behar, comp., *Las guerras de la paz*, pp. 267–75. The fact that "Antonio" ended up working for Colombian intelligence does not make his account of life in the FARC in the 1970s less convincing.

167 Alfredo Molano, "Fórmulas." The most thorough examination of the peace process is Mark Chernick, "Insurgency and Negotiations: Defining the Boundaries of the Political Regime in Colombia," Ph.D. Dissertation, Columbia University, 1991. For primary sources, see Behar, comp., *Las guerras de la paz*.

168 In the Cauca in the mid-1980s, FARC and military-paramilitary violence against indigenous communities led to the formation of a regional guerrilla group, Quintín Lame, which laid down its arms in 1991.

169 Relations between the FARC and the ELN varied over time and according to region. In 2005, in some areas, such as southern Bolívar or the Sierra Nevada de Santa Marta, the FARC and the ELN carried out joint attacks on paramilitary bases, while in eastern Antioquia and Arauca, the FARC declared war on the ELN.

170 Kirk, *More Terrible than Death*, p. 152. Committed at night by men dressed as civilians and wearing hoods, twenty more massacres had followed in Urabá by 1990.

171 It left 43 people dead and 50 injured in one evening. There were 154 soldiers bunkered down in the Batallón Bombona. In 1983, Fidel Castaño had been accused of massacring 20 people in Remedios and Segovia at a time when he and Carlos served as informants for said battalion.

172 Romero, *Paramilitares*, pp. 200–201.

173 Dudley, *Walking Ghosts*, pp. 111–12, 147. In Meta, in coordination with the army's VII Brigade in Villavicencio, paramilitaries working for emerald czars Rodríguez and Victor Carranza assassinated 142 UP militants and disappeared 11 in 1988 alone.

174 Escobar's political godfather, Alberto Santofimio, was arrested in May 2005 on charges of being the intellectual author of the hit, after Escobar's security chief, John Jairo Velásquez Vásquez, a.k.a. "Popeye," offered testimony to the prosecutor's office. *BBC News*, 12 May 2005. In 1994, Luis Carlos Aguilar, a.k.a. "El Mugre," who drove Santofimio to the meeting with Escobar, had done the same. *El Tiempo*, 16 May 2005.

175 For a chilling account of Carlos Castaño's open admission of responsibility for both Jaramillo and Pizarro's murders, see Dudley, *Walking Ghosts*, pp. 203–204. M-19 and the UP had been moving toward unity beyond the reach of the FARC.

176 *Ibid.*, p. 151.

Fragmented Peace, Parcellized Sovereignty: 1990–98

177 William Avilés, "Paramilitarism and Colombia's Low-Intensity Democracy," *Journal of Latin American Studies* 38 (2006), pp. 381–4.

178 Colombia," *Análisis Político* 19 (Mayo–Agosto 1993), pp. 3–22. Two years later, in 1993, Afro-Colombians obtained similar rights under Law 70.

179 Economist Intelligence Unit, *Colombia: Country Profile, 2002–2003* (London 2003).

180 Romero, *Paramilitares*, pp. 178–89.

181 *Ibid.*, p. 346; Camilo Castellanos, "A la nueva república le falta sujeto," in Castellanos et al., *Colombia: Análisis al futuro* (Bogotá 1992), pp. 9–28.

182 For the fate of M-19, EPL, and Quintín Lame, see Ricardo Peñaranda and Javier Guerrero, *De las armas a la política* (Bogotá 1999); Lawrence Boudon, "Colombia's M-19 Democratic Alliance: A Case Study in New-Party Self-Destruction," *Latin American Perspectives* 116 (28: 1) (January 2001), pp. 73–92.

183 *Idem*, "Introduction: Prospects for Peace," in Bergquist et al., eds, *Violence in Colombia, 1990–2000*, pp. 25–9.

184 Sánchez, "Guerra prolongada y negociaciones inciertas," p. 61.

185 Sebastian Edwards, *The Economics and Politics of Transition to an Open Market Economy: Colombia*, OECD Report 2001, pp. 39–41 and Table 3.3.

186 Richani, *Systems of Violence*, pp. 101–109. See also, Francisco Thoumi, *La economía política del narcotráfico* (Bogotá 1994).

187 In *ibid.*, p. 196, n. 53, a rentier economy is defined as "one where capital

formation is mainly based on the extraction of natural resources and land speculation . . . and with the . . . development of the trade infrastructure as opposed to a diversified economy based on the production of goods. Free trade and the incorporation process into global markets facilitate rentier economies."

188 Mark Bowden, *Killing Pablo: The Hunt for the World's Greatest Outlaw* (New York 2002).
189 Escobar considered himself a man of the Left, a foe of imperialism and the oligarchy, had ties to M-19 in the early 1980s and to the ELN in the early 1990s. Salazar, *La parábola de Pablo*, pp. 85–7, 103, 268.
190 See William Ramírez Tobón, "¿Un campesino ilítico?" *Análisis Político* 29 (Septiembre–Diciembre 1996), pp. 67–72.
191 Richani, *Systems of Violence*, p. 145.
192 For the colonization of Guaviare and Vaupés, see Molano, *Selva Adentro*; and of Vichada and Guainía, *idem, Aguas Arriba* (Bogotá 1990). The history of the coca frontier is explored in William Ramírez Tobón, "La guerrilla rural en Colombia: ¿Una vía hacia la colonización armada?," *Estudios Rurales Latinoamericanos*, vol. 4, no. 2 (1981), pp. 199–209; Fernando Cubides et al., *Colonización, coca, y guerrilla* (Bogotá 1989); Alfredo Molano, "Algunas consideraciones sobre colonización y violencia," in Catherine LeGrand et al., comps, *El agro y la cuestión social* (Bogotá 1994), pp. 27–41; and for a summary of the debate, LeGrand, "Colonización y violencia en Colombia: Perspectivas y debate," in *El agro y la cuestión social.*
193 Ricardo Rocha García, *La economía colombiana tras 25 años de narcotráfico* (Bogotá 2000), p. 143.
194 Richani, *Systems of Violence*, p. 71.
195 "The Letter of the Intellectuals," in Bergquist et al., eds, *Violence in Colombia, 1990–2000*, pp. 214–16. For the guerrilla response, see *ibid.*, pp. 216–20. See also, Gonzalo Sánchez, "A Response to the Guerrillas," in *ibid.*, pp. 220–23, originally published in *El Espectador.*
196 For Caquetá, see Juan Guillermo Ferro Medina, "Las FARC y su relación con la economía de la coca en el sur de Colombia: Testimonios de colonos y guerrilleros," in Sánchez and Lair, comps, *Violencias y estrategias colectivas en la región andina*, pp. 411–42. The FARC was initially opposed to coca cultivation, but the desperate economic situation of frontier settlers convinced them it would have to be tolerated.
197 María Victoria Uribe, *Limpiar la tierra: Guerra entre esmeralderos* (Bogotá 1992).
198 The number of FARC fronts is taken from Sánchez, "Guerra prolongada y negociaciones inciertas," p. 41.
199 Unlike the FARC, the ELN benefited minimally from the narco-economy – a legacy of its background in liberation theology. Coca plantations flourished in ELN-influenced areas in southern Bolívar and the Catatumbo Mountains of Northern Santander, which were taken over by the AUC in the late 1990s.
200 Fernando Cubides, *Burocracias armadas* (Bogotá 2005). See also, Francisco

Gutiérrez, "Prólogo," in Juan Guillermo Ferro Medina and Graciela Uribe Ramón, *El orden de la guerra: Las FARC-EP entre la organización y la política* (Bogotá 2002), p. 10.

201 Richani, *Systems of Violence*, p. 148.

202 Ferro Medina and Uribe Ramón, *El orden de la guerra*, pp. 66–74. Peasant women find paths of upward mobility through greater command of basic literacy and communications technology.

203 Richani, *Systems of Violence*, p. 184, n. 23.

204 The phrase is taken from Fernando Cubides, "From Public to Private Violence," in Bergquist et al., eds, *Violence in Colombia, 1990–2000*, p. 133. On multinational corporations and paramilitaries, see Richani, *Systems of Violence*, pp. 113–16; and Livingstone, *Inside Colombia*, pp. 80–99.

205 Antioquia is one of three departments – along with the Chocó to the south and Córdoba to the north – in which Urabá is located.

206 *El Tiempo*, 28 September 1997.

207 *El Tiempo*, 26–28 January 2005; *Semana*, 30 January 2005; *El Espectador*, 6 February 2006; "El secreto de los militares," *Semana*, 6 February 2005. For a more detailed description of the massacre, see Kirk, *More Terrible than Death*, pp. 250–56. In March 2005, the Inter-American Human Rights Court of the OAS declared the Colombian state responsible for the Mapiripán massacre. Along with Carlos Castaño and another paramilitary leader, Colonel Lino Sánchez was sentenced to forty years, while the sergeant in charge of the San José airport received a thirty-two-year sentence. Uscátegui and Orozco served forty and thirty-eight months, respectively.

208 Livingstone, *Inside Colombia*, p. 10.

209 Richani, *Systems of Violence*, p. 120.

210 Kirk, *More Terrible than Death*, pp. 192–3. Bedoya, for whom Human Rights Watch was an organization "in the direct pay" of the FARC, resigned in 1997 after President Samper's refusal to take further repressive measures against the coca growers' movement.

211 Quoted in Romero, *Paramilitares*, p. 195.

212 Quoted in *ibid.*, p. 218.

213 Kirk, *More Terrible than Death*, p. 194. After filing a report about Del Río's involvement with paramilitaries, Velásquez was dismissed by General Bedoya for lack of *esprit de corps*.

214 Romero, *Paramilitares*, p. 181.

215 Alfredo Molano, "División Creadora," *El Espectador*, 8 February 2003.

216 The peace community movement in Urabá began in the late 1980s, when Fidel Castaño's paramilitary *Tangueros*, led by younger brother Carlos, massacred civilians and dispossessed communities for supporting the UP.

217 *Ibid.*, pp. 212–14.

Involution, 1998–2002

218 Sánchez, "Guerra prolongada y negociaciones inciertas," p. 64.

219 Ferro Medina and Uribe Ramón, *El orden de la guerra*, pp. 129–30.

220 Omar Gutiérrez, "La oposición regional a las negociaciones con el ELN," *Análisis Político* 52 (Septiembre–Diciembre), pp. 34–50. The ELN's image was badly damaged by pipeline sabotage that killed seventy people in Machuca, Antioquia in 1998.

221 Livingstone, *Inside Colombia*, pp. 24–5. The ELN had highjacked a commercial airliner in Venezuela in 1999 and kidnapped an entire church congregation in Cali in 2000, while the FARC began its "miracle fishing" expeditions, setting up random roadblocks throughout the country in hopes of encountering "kidnappable people" (*secuestrables*).

222 In *Systems of Violence*, p. 35, Richani writes: "The new fault line of conflict that started taking shape in the 1980s is between a rentier economy and a . . . peasant economy represented by poor peasants, colonos, and indigenous and Afro-Colombian communities whose lands became the target of speculators . . . and multinational companies."

223 Many ELN gains from the period 1983–96 were wiped out by 2000. It was effectively dislodged from traditional bases in northeastern Antioquia and southern Bolívar, where it had long regulated coca production, as well as market relations between small gold miners, merchants, and foreign capital; the Catatumbo region of Northern Santander, where it regulated the coca market; the Cimitarra Valley in Santander, where the group was born; and cities like Cúcuta, Bucaramanga, and Barrancabermeja – ELN fiefdoms until the late 1990s.

224 Bruce Bagley, "Drug Trafficking, Political Violence, and US Policy in Colombia in the 1990s" (2001): www.mamacoca.org. The FARC worked through the kingpin of Rio's favelas, Fernandinho, whose liaison, "El Negro Acacio," the FARC's own cocaine lord, ran independent production facilities and transport routes through Venezuela, Guyana, and northern Brazil. He was the first of a series of FARC commanders wanted for extradition to the USA on trafficking charges. At large at the time of writing, he had become the stuff of legend and folklore along the Colombian border with Venezuela.

225 In June 2005, McCaffrey was sent to assess prospects for US occupation and counterinsurgency in Iraq.

226 Angel Rabasa and Peter Chalk, *Colombian Labyrinth: The Synergy of Drugs and Insurgency and its Implications for Regional Stability* (Santa Monica 2001).

227 Gabriel Marcella, *Plan Colombia: Strategic and Operational Imperatives* (Santa Monica 2001).

228 Aijaz Ahmad, "Colombia's Lethal Concoction," *Frontline* (Delhi), 7 April 2006, p. 59.

229 Adam Isacson, "Number Three No More," 19 April 2005: www. ciponline.org.

230 Quoted in Isacson, "John Kerry's Statement," 15 October 2004: www. ciponline.org.

231 Unlike the ELN, the FARC wanted drilling to go ahead on U'wa territory, in order to extract protection rents from Occidental. The FARC had previously executed ELN combatants for supporting U'wa demands. Kirk, *More Terrible than Death*, p. 227.

232 *Ibid.*, p. 260. For an analysis of Plan Colombia's failures, see Adam Isacson, "Putumayo, 5 Years into Plan Colombia," 1 August 2005: www. ciponline.org; *idem*, "Did Plan Colombia Work? A Look at the Numbers," 18 January 2006: www.democracyarsenal.org.

233 Sánchez, "Guerra prolongada y negociaciones inciertas," p. 50.

234 See Garry Leech, *Killing Peace: Colombia's Conflict and the Failure of US Intervention* (New York 2001).

235 *El Tiempo*, 18 January 1997. Quoted in Mauricio Romero, "Democratización política y contra reforma paramilitar en Colombia," in Sánchez and Lair, comps, *Violencias y estrategias colectivas*, p. 367.

236 Quoted in Kirk, *More Terrible than Death*, p. 193.

237 Garry Leech, "Reinventing Carlos Castaño," 30 September 2002: www.colombiajournal.org; Jaime Zuluaga Nieto, "Del paramilitarismo a la parapolítica," *El Espectador*, 24 July 2005.

238 *El Tiempo*, 19 May 2005; "Investigarán relación de congresistas y 'paras'," *El País*, 20 May 2005; "Uribe niega tener vínculos con los 'paras' de derecha," *El Nuevo Herald* (Miami), 22 May 2005; Gonzalo Guillén, "Acusan a Uribe de proteger a un hermano y a dos primos, presuntamente asesinos," *El Nuevo Herald*, 23 June 2005.

239 Fabio Castillo, *Los jinetes de la cocaína* (Bogotá 1987), p. 72. Castillo was a three-time winner of the Simón Bolívar Award, Colombia's most prestigious investigative journalism prize. He focused mainly on Uribe Sierra in his discussion of right-wing narcotraffickers, but also mentioned Uribe Vélez.

240 Joseph Contreras, with the collaboration of Fernando Garavito, *El Señor de las Sombras: Biografía no autorizada de Álvaro Uribe Vélez* (Bogotá 2000), pp. 35–43, 65–72, 92, 167. Contreras was *Newsweek*'s Latin American editor; Garavito, a Colombian political columnist driven into exile by paramilitary threats.

241 Jeremy Bigwood, "Doing the US's Dirty Work: The Colombian Paramilitaries and Israel," citing a 1998 DEA Report: www.narconews.com. For Molano, see "Peor el remedio," *El Espectador*, 1 September 2002.

242 Romero, *Paramilitares*, pp. 193–4.

243 In 2005, the case against General del Río was dismissed. Antonio Caballero, "Amenazas, malentendidos, y malas compañías," *Semana*, July 2005; Ramiro Bejarano Guzmán, "El amigo secreto," *El Espectador*, 3 July 2005; Gerardo Reyes and Gonzalo Guillén, "Amistad con un narco pone

en aprietos a Uribe," *El Nuevo Herald,* 5 July 2005; Adam Isacson, "President Uribe's Shady Friend," 12 July 2005: www.ciponline.org. See also, Contreras y Garavito, *El Señor de las Sombras,* p. 62.

The Edge of the Precipice, 2002–5

244 Alfredo Molano predicted this in "El día antes," *El Espectador,* 14 May 2000. For all this, see also, Mario Murillo, *Colombia and the United States: War, Terrorism, and Destabilization* (New York 2004).
245 See Carlos Castaño, *Mi confesión* (Bogotá 2001).
246 See Human Rights Watch, "State of War: Political Violence and Counter-insurgency in Colombia" (1993); "Colombia's Killer Networks: The Military-Paramilitary Partnership and the United States" (1996); "The 'Sixth Division': Military-Paramilitary Ties and US Policy in Colombia" (2001); "Colombia: Letting the Paramilitaries off the Hook" (2005): www.hrw.org.
247 *El Tiempo,* 27 March 2002. According to former Interior Minister Armando Estrada, candidates sympathetic to paramilitaries gained a third of congressional and Senate seats.
248 US foreign policy took a momentary turn against the paramilitaries in February 2004, and, following the pattern set by his brother Fidel in 1994, Carlos Castaño "disappeared" in April 2004. Eerily, Carlos, who had compared himself to Houdini in his autobiography, predicted his own vanishing act in an interview with a US journalist. In another context, a political counselor from the US Embassy predicted to a human rights investigator that Castaño would disappear once his mission had been accomplished. See Dudley, *Walking Ghosts,* pp. 198, 206; Kirk, *More Terrible than Death,* p. 247.
249 *El Tiempo,* 12 February 2005.
250 *El Tiempo,* 23 May 2005.
251 Alfredo Molano, "Sentando Bases," October 2004: www.mamacoca.org.
252 Adam Isacson, "Peace – or 'Paramilitarization'?" July 2005: www.ciponline.org.
253 *Idem,* "Paramilitarism's Inexorable Progress," 28 March 2005: www.ciponline.org.
254 *El Tiempo,* 20 July 2005.
255 Adam Isacson, "Don Berna in Custody," 31 May 2005: www.ciponline.org.
256 Garry Leech, "An Unjust Demobilization," 20 June 2005: www.colombiajournal.org.
257 *El Tiempo,* 2 July 2005.
258 *Vanguardia Liberal,* 19 July 2005.
259 Álvaro Delgado, "El problema de fondo," *Actualidad Colombiana* XXVI: 405 (27 April 2005).
260 José Miguel Vivanco and Maria McFarland Sánchez-Moreno, "A Bad Plan

in Colombia," *International Herald Tribune*, 16 May 2005. The UN agreed, though with typically bland circumspection. In "Colombia's Paramilitaries," *International Herald Tribune*, 31 May 2005, Colombian Chancellor Barco asserted, "I can think of no similar process in modern history that has been as democratic and open to free and frank debate by all interested parties." Like the AUC, Barco excluded victims of paramilitary atrocities from the list of "interested parties." This violated international law, as the José Alvear Restrepo Lawyers' Collective, among others, pointed out.

261 Álvaro Camacho Guizado, "Paras y parapolítica," *El Espectador*, 12 June 2005. "Violentology" is an interdisciplinary field that has acted as the center of gravity of history and the social sciences in Colombia since the 1980s. Camacho is a pioneering sociologist of politics, organized crime, and urban violence.

262 Javier Zuluaga Nieto, "Del paramilitarismo a la parapolítica."

263 2005; John Otis, "Colombia might sacrifice justice in search of peace," *Houston Chronicle*, 21 May 2005; Alfredo Molano, "Delete," *El Espectador*, 22 May 2005.

264 *El Nuevo Herald*, 14 June 2005.

265 *Semana*, 10 October 2004.

266 In July 2005, Uribe led a diplomatic tour to Madrid and London to hawk the scheme, calculating, correctly as it turned out, that he would find Trojan Horses on Europe's periphery through which to smuggle demobilization onto the EU foreign policy agenda. In an otherwise uncritical discussion of the fight against terrorism in London, Madrid, and Bogotá, the *Financial Times* acknowledged that "some European politicians" had highlighted connections between the Colombian Army and paramilitaries.

267 "Secretario del Ministerio de Defensa alemán expresa su respaldo a Política de Seguridad Democrática:" www.mindefensa.gov.co.

268 For the failure of initial demobilizations, see Human Rights Watch, "Smoke and Mirrors: Colombia's Demobilization of Paramilitary Groups" (2005): www.hrw.org; UN High Commissioner for Human Rights Office in Colombia, "Consideraciones sobre la ley de 'Justicia y Paz'," 27 June 2005.

269 Quoted in Luis Jaime Acosta, "Feared Colombian militias want political party," Reuters, 21 July 2005.

270 "No voy a volver al monte," *Semana*, 16 April 2005; Jaime Zuluaga Nieto, "Del paramilitarismo a la parapolítica."

271 For an early analysis of paramilitary rhetoric, see Fernando Estrada Gallego, "La retórica de paramilitarismo: Análisis del discurso en el conflicto armado," *Análisis Político* 44 (Septiembre–Diciembre 2001), pp. 44–66.

272 *Semana*, 5 June 2005.

273 Although Murillo did not hold office from his prison cell in a suburb south of Medellín, he managed real – as opposed to formal – power in Medellín. This was demonstrated in late May 2005, when Colombian authorities began their "manhunt" for him, the largest since the death of Pablo Escobar, and transport workers paralyzed Medellín in response. Unsurpris-

ingly, unlike trade unionists, Murillo's transport workers did not face high-level state and paramilitary violence.

274 Jerry Seper, "U.S. seeks Colombian Rebels' Extradition," *Washington Times*, 18 April 2006.

275 Forrest Hylton, "Colombia: Politics as Organized Crime?" *NACLA Report on the Americas* (May–June 2006).

276 Héctor-León Moncayo, "Las Máscaras del Poder," *Le Monde Diplomatique-Colombia* (July 2002), pp. 4–5; Alfredo Molano, "República Ganadera," *El Espectador*, 10 November 2002.

277 Codhes, "¿Penas, tierras y extradición?": www.codhes.org.co; "¿Hasta Cuándo?" *El Tiempo*, 13 June 2005.

278 For some of those stories, see Alfredo Molano, *The Dispossessed: Los Desterrados of Colombia* (Chicago 2005). For statistics, see Darío Fajardo, "Tierra, poder político y reforma agraria," ILSA (Bogotá 2002), cited in Moncayo, "Las máscaras del poder;" Alfredo Molano, "Políticas enlatadas," *El Espectador*, 24 November 2002.

279 "Autodefensas se apropiaron de las tierras en Urabá por la fuerza," *El Tiempo*, 2 July 2005. In San Pedro de Urabá, where the Mapiripán massacre had been planned, the AUC made an offer few married male homesteaders could have refused: "Do you want to sell to us, or do we buy it from your widow later?" Potential buyers in Urabá were all from "the enterprise" – code for the AUC (borrowed, incidentally, from the insurgencies).

280 For fumigation, see Hugh O'Shaughnessy and Sue Branford, *Chemical Warfare in Colombia: The Costs of Coca Fumigation* (London 2005).

281 "Colombia's Politics," *The Economist*, 5 June 2003.

282 Alfredo Molano, "Fumigación de parques," *El Espectador*, 17 December 2003; *idem*, "A dos fuegos," *El Espectador*, 1 May 2005.

283 T. Christian Miller, "Major Cocaine Source Wanes," *Los Angeles Times*, 8 June 2003.

284 Darío González Vargas, "Armas químicas y biológicas en el Plan Colombia. Interrogantes sobre 'la estrategia antinarcóticos'," in Estrada Álvarez, comp., *El Plan Colombia y la intensificación de la guerra: Aspectos globales y locales*, pp. 421–49.

285 Alfredo Molano, "A dos fuegos."

War as Peace, 2005–6

286 Eduardo Pizarro Leongómez, *Una democracia asediada: Balance y perspectivas del conflicto armado en Colombia* (Bogotá 2004); Francisco Leal, "La seguridad durante el primer año del gobierno de Álvaro Uribe Vélez," *Análisis Político* 50 (Enero–Abril 2004), p. 96, writes, "Any peace process has to do with the interpretation of armed conflict, and if this is erroneous, costly errors are made." For a look at Uribe's first year in government that examines the practical consequences of flawed interpretations, see Daniel Pécaut, *Midiendo fuerzas* (Bogotá 2003).

287 José Obdulio Gaviria, *Los sofismas de la guerra en Colombia* (Bogotá 2004). Gaviria, cousin of the late Pablo Escobar, is a former Left-Liberal turned right-wing ideologue. For discussion of how to name the current phase of war, see Pécaut, *Guerra contra la sociedad*; Eduardo Posada Carbó, *¿Guerra civil? El lenguaje del conflicto colombiano* (Bogotá 2001); Álvaro Camacho Guizado "Credo, necesidad y codicia: los alimentos de la guerra," William Ramírez Tobón "¿Guerra civil en Colombia?", and Eduardo Pizarro Leongómez "Colombia: ¿guerra civil, guerra contra la sociedad, guerra antiterrorista o guerra ambigua?" in *Análisis Político* 46 (Mayo–Agosto 2002), pp. 137–80; Eric Lair, "El terror, recurso estratégico de los actores armados en Colombia," in *Guerra en Colombia* (Bogotá 2004), pp. 131–9; and Eduardo Pizarro, "¿Conflicto armado o amenaza terrorista?" *El Tiempo*, 26 April 2005.

288 Kirk, *More Terrible than Death*, p. 99. The insight belongs to Antonio Caballero.

289 Isabel Hilton, "Colombia's Drug Untouchables," *The Guardian*, 13 July 2005.

290 Romero, *Paramilitares*, pp. 235–7. See also, Pécaut, *Midiendo fuerzas*; Christian Parenti, *The Freedom: Shadows and Hallucinations in Occupied Iraq* (New York 2004), p. 206; Greg Grandin, *Empire's Workshop: Latin America and the Roots of US Imperialism* (New York 2006).

291 Eduardo Pizarro, quoted in Kirk, *More Terrible than Death*, p. 113.

292 See Adam Isacson, "San José de Apartadó: Jesús Abad's disturbing account," 1 April 2005: www.ciponline.org.

293 Bill Weinberg, "In Colombia, Indigenous Peace Initiatives under Attack," Pacific News Service, 17 June 2005: news.pacificnews.org. On 9 March 2005, thirty-two US Congresspersons, including Republican leaders of the House and the Senate, sent President Uribe a letter expressing concern that along with local paramilitaries, members of XI and XVII brigades may have been involved. The head of the XVII Brigade, General Hector Jaime Fandiño Rincón, had studied at the School of the Americas during the era of Plan Cóndor. In a letter dated 1 July 2005, Democrat Patrick Leahy and Republican Richard Lugar, head of the Senate Foreign Relations Committee, along with twenty other senators, urged US Secretary of State Condoleezza Rice not to certify the Uribe administration for progress in human rights. They cited the massacre in San José, among other atrocities. Adam Isacson, "Human Rights Certification? Not Yet," 16 July 2005: www.ciponline.org.

294 In response, the UN High Commission reminded Uribe that the Inter-American Human Rights Court of the OAS required the Colombian government to guarantee the security of all members of peace communities. *El Tiempo*, 23 March 2005.

295 Hugh Bronstein, "Police in, Population out after Colombian Massacre," Reuters, 10 May 2005; Winifred Tate, "A Visit to San José de Apartadó," 13 June 2005: www.ciponline.org; Comunicado Público de la Comunidad

de Paz de San José de Apartadó, "La verdad y la transparencia no son ambigüedad ni confusión," 14 June 2005: www.codhes.org.co; Colombia Support Network, "The Massacre at Mulatos in Colombia," 26 June 2005: http://colombiasupport.net.

296 Headwaters from five rivers came together in San José: the Apartadó, Carepa, Currulao, Mulatos, and Riogrande.

297 *Semana,* 5 June 2005.

298 Molano, "¿Qué hay detrás de San José?" *El Espectador,* 12 March 2005; Community Council of Curvaradó y Jiguamiandó, "Avanza la palma, la siembra ilegal con la complicidad de la Brigada 17," 21 July 2005: http://colombiaindymedia.org. Above-mentioned rivers are situated in the part of Urabá belonging to the Chocó.

299 Comunicado Público de la Comunidad de Paz de San José de Apartadó, "La verdad y la transparencia no son ambigüedad ni confusión."

300 Justin Podur, "Will People Power Have a Chance?" 23 April 2005: www.zmag.org.

301 Bill Weinberg, "In Colombia."

302 *Vanguardia Liberal,* 7 July 2005.

303 In 1985, Tacueyó was the site of the most gruesome guerrilla massacre to date. In the grip of paranoia, the commander of the Rodrigo Franco Front, composed of FARC dissidents close to M-19, liquidated some 180 of his own soldiers, many of them Nasa.

304 Karl Penhaul, "Colombia troops take rebel-held town," 28 April 2005: www.cnn.com. Juan Forero, "Colombia War Spills into Indians' Peaceful World," *New York Times,* 2 May 2005.

305 "Uribe ordena una guerra sin cuartel para aplastar a las FARC," *El Nuevo Herald,* 1 May 2005.

306 For a critique of the military efficacy of democratic security policies, see Francisco Leal, "La seguridad durante el primer año del gobierno de Álvaro Uribe Vélez," *Análisis Político* 50 (Enero–Abril 2004), pp. 97–8.

307 For a capsule summary of FARC relations with indigenous peoples in Cauca, see Richani, *Systems of Violence,* p. 188, n. 15; Pablo Tattay, "FARC y población indígena: Una muestra de la relación con la población civil," in *Las verdaderas intenciones de las FARC* (Bogotá 1999), pp. 194–8. Tattay was the spokesman for the Quintín Lame guerrilla group in negotiations with the Gaviria government.

308 *El Tiempo,* 19 May 2005.

309 *El Tiempo,* 3 May 2005.

310 "Indígenas dejan consejo por diferencias con el Presidente," *El Colombiano,* 1 May 2005.

311 Quoted in "No vamos a obedecerle a nadie," *Vanguardia Liberal,* 3 May 2005.

312 Adam Isacson, "Clear and Hold," 5 January 2006: www.ciponline.org.

Conclusion: Amnesia by Decree[313]

313 On amnesia, see Antonio Caballero, "Prólogo," in Behar, comp., *Las guerras de la paz*, pp. 7–9.

314 Noam Chomsky, *At War with Asia: Essays on Indochina* (New York 1972), p. 55; Mike Davis, *Planet of Slums* (New York 2006), p. 56.

315 Fabio López de la Roche, "Cultura política de las clases dirigentes en Colombia," p. 181.

316 Alfredo Molano, "La tierra es para quien la expropria," *El Espectador*, 17 October 2004.

317 For China's state-led process, which relies on debt and taxation rather than violent expropriation, see Yiang Lin, "Dark Side of the Chinese Moon," *New Left Review* 32 (March–April 2005), pp. 131–40.

318 For a cautionary note regarding the legacy of *la Violencia*, see Álvaro Camacho Guizado, "El ayer y el hoy de la violencia en Colombia: Continuidades y descontinuidades," *Análisis Político* 12 (Enero–Abril 1991), pp. 27–42.

319 Sánchez, "Reseña: *Orden y Violencia*, por Daniel Pécaut," *Análisis Político* 2 (Septiembre–Diciembre 1987), p. 164.

320 *Idem*, "Guerra prolongada y negociaciones inciertas," p. 25.

321 William I. Robinson, *Transnational Conflicts: Central America, Social Change, and Globalization* (New York 2003).

322 Greg Grandin, "The Instruction of Great Catastrophe: Truth Commissions, National History, and State Formation in Argentina, Chile, and Guatemala," *American Historical Review* 110: 1 (February 2005), pp. 46–67. For a comparative study of truth comissions and legislation on crimes against humanity, see Iván Cepeda Castro and Claudia Girón Ortiz, "Procesos públicos de esclarecimiento y justicia de crímenes contra la humanidad," *Análisis Político* 50 (Enero–Abril 2004), pp. 52–71.

Index